Are You Ready to Believe?

David Holt

INNER CROW
PUBLISHING

PHOENIX, ARIZONA

Inner Crow Publishing
Phoenix, Arizona
www.AreYouReadytoBelieve.com

Book Layout ©2013 BookDesignTemplates.com

Cover Photo: Kirk Mottershead

Are You Ready to Believe?/ David Holt. —1st ed.
ISBN 978-0-9932896-0-6

Contents

Dedication

To Spirit

Without their influence, this book would not have been possible

Acknowledgments:

I would like to thank my wife, Jane, for putting up with me,

my editor, Kit, for all her hard work,

and Alan

I would also like to thank all those who shared their stories and experiences with me

Introduction

Spirit have always been there. They have been with me since the day I was born, watching, waiting and guiding my life from the other side. It's a perfect partnership. I pass on their messages and bridge the gap between the two worlds. And they . . . well, they pretty much take care of everything in my life. This partnership that Spirit and I share together has taken me on an amazing journey and one I'd like to share with you.

My experiences over the years have opened my eyes to a new way of thinking, a new way of living, and more importantly a new way of viewing the process that we call death.

The reason I wrote *Are You Ready to Believe?* is to help people understand exactly what it is I do in my role as a medium. I'd like to give you an insight into my world and leave you with a true understanding of what it means to be a medium.

There is an unseen world that surrounds us, and in that world is everyone you have ever loved and lost. The moment you think about someone on the other side, they are with you.

Over the many years that I have worked as a medium, the one question I am asked more than any other is, "Are they okay?"

The insight I have into the spirit world can answer this question in just one word, *yes*. Your loved ones in the spirit world are okay, and yes, you will see them again.

But don't take my word for it. Read on and hear from just a few of the many thousands of people I've read for. Their relatives tell the story far better than I can.

"Your loved ones are only a thought away."

~David Holt

CHAPTER 1

The Woman with Black Hair

The woman walked through the dim hallway of the small terraced house glancing into rooms downstairs. No one was around. Both the living room and the kitchen were empty of people. She realized that it was the end of the day and the small family was settling in for the night.

Up the narrow stairway, across the tiny landing, the woman moved to the larger of the three bedrooms upstairs. A man and a woman were sound asleep in the double bed. They slumbered peacefully. She watched them for a moment, then moved on.

She made no sound as she went along the narrow hallway of the tiny home and stood in the doorway of one of the bedrooms where a little boy slept.

Inside the bedroom was a bed tucked away in the corner and in it, she could see a little boy with rosy cheeks and fair hair. The boy had been playing with his toys still scattered over the floor where he'd left them before climbing into bed.

The boy was about four-years-old.

He made a small lump underneath the covers, moving restlessly, trying to find the perfect position to finally go to sleep.

The woman stepped inside the room, looking even more closely at the little boy.

When she reached the side of his bed, his eyes popped open. She could see the dim light from the hallway reflected in them.

He appeared to be staring directly at her.

That was impossible.

No one had been able to see her. Not for a very long time. Perhaps he heard something, or needed a glass of water.

Just then, the little boy opened his mouth and screamed.

Immediately, the boy's mother burst into the room.

"What? What's wrong?" Her hair was messed, her eyes wild. What was wrong with her little boy?

He sobbed and clung to her. "I saw a lady. She was right there. It was a stranger."

"Shh, shh. There's no one there. It was just a dream. Go back to sleep."

The boy heard his mother quickly go downstairs and check the front door. Then she came back up and paused for a moment in his doorway, watching him, before heading back to bed, satisfied that he seemed to be quiet again.

The instant he heard his mother go back to bed, the boy's eyes popped open. He lay there for a very long time, watching the doorway.

But the woman had vanished.

CHAPTER 2

Early Experiences

That little boy was me and it was the very first time I remember seeing someone who had crossed over into the spirit world. The next morning I couldn't stop talking about the woman I had seen standing at the side of my bed. My mother recalled how I would waken in the night on other occasions and that I had also mentioned seeing people in my room.

As a way of pacifying me, she always reassured me by saying they were nothing more than dreams.

But my persistence in talking about this woman and describing her in great detail got my parents' attention.

"It sounds like he's describing Kathleen, my first wife," my stepfather said.

He searched for an old photo album. From it, he produced a black and white photo of a pretty lady with long black hair. They both looked at the picture before showing it to me.

I felt a shock of recognition run through me.

"That's her!" I shouted.

The description of the stranger in my room I had given countless times that morning described in every detail the woman in the picture.

The lady I had seen was undeniably my stepfather's first wife, Kathleen.

She had died when she was just thirty-three years old, many years before my mother and stepfather had met.

"It sounds like he's seen a ghost."

My parents were right; I had seen a ghost, or more precisely, a spirit.

Although my first experience with a spirit person had startled me, I'm pretty sure that was not their intention. Spirit people are around us all the time but they just aren't used to being seen.

I was a young child who had "Don't talk to strangers" drummed into me. When a stranger unexpectedly appeared in my bedroom that night, I gave the appropriate reaction.

Although she was the first spirit person I can recall seeing, the woman with black hair was just the start of things to come.

❧❧

My arrival into this world was rather a difficult one.

When my mother was pregnant and expecting my younger brother, Martin, she wanted to have a home birth. In order to do this in Bolton, she had to clear it with her doctor and midwife.

After checking her records, the midwife responded with, "We're sorry, but due to all the complications you had with your first child, you won't be able to have a home birth."

Determined to have a home birth, my mother pressed for answers. "I know he was born breech, but other than that he was okay."

The midwife said, "I'm afraid you can't have a home birth because your first child, David, had to be resuscitated."

"What? I wasn't told anything about this." My mother was shocked and surprised.

This was the first she'd heard of it, three years after my birth. If I had been an only child perhaps she would never have known about the resuscitation. I have my brother's arrival to thank for that.

At the time of my birth, she had no previous experience with the birthing process, so to have me whisked away for several hours didn't seem altogether unusual.

When I was finally placed in her arms, they didn't mention the difficulties they'd had with my arrival, or the fact they had to re-suscitate me.

On July 5th 1983 at 1:45am, I was born, I died, and then came back.

It would appear that I have been connected with the spirit world from the very beginning.

❧

It is only when I look back on my childhood experiences that I realize Spirit has always been present and playing a part in my life. At the time, I didn't associate the unusual happenings with the spirit world. All I knew is that every so often something unusual or even spooky would happen. My ability to connect with Spirit was present, but simply unrecognized for what it was.

One in a Million

As a young child, we often had family holidays at the famed Golden Sands Holiday Camp, in Rhyl, North Wales. I had been enjoying a weeklong holiday with my grandparents.

At this time, I developed an interest in dinosaurs, mainly through school and various TV programs. My grandad was an avid mineral collector and was always adding to his rather impressive collection of rocks, crystals, and gem stones. If there were a mineral shop to be found on holiday, you'd be sure to find him in there.

The night before we were due to go home, he was looking at a crystal he had treated himself to. He marveled at the millions of years it took for such things to form. After I brought up the subject of dinosaurs, he explained how fossils form over millions of years and about the specialist rock tapping equipment needed to find them.

The next morning I was up, dressed, and ready to go on the beach just one last time.

"You'll have to be quick, we're loading the car soon, so hurry up back," Nana said.

I ran to the beach as fast as I could for one last look at the sea. The beach in Rhyl is covered by thousands upon thousands of pebbles. As I wandered out onto the pebbles, the thought of dinosaurs and fossils filled my mind. I wanted to go on a fossil hunt.

"Come on Love, we're almost ready now," Nana shouted.

"Okay."

My time was up. I walked across the pebbles and up the concrete steps to the road, but the urge to run back just one last time and stand on the beach overcame me.

I ran back down the concrete steps and onto the pebbles. I wanted a pebble to take back home with me, but which one? There were thousands of them. There wasn't time to think, so I grabbed the first one I set eyes on. It was just the perfect size to fit into the palm of my hand, and to my absolute amazement when I turned it over it was a fossil!

A fossil of a leaf.

Excited, I ran to my grandad as quickly as I could, "Look, look, Grandad, I've found a fossil!!!"

"Bloody hell, where did you get that from? That's a fossil!" Grandad said.

Each year we returned to the beach at Golden Sands, and each year I looked for another fossil. To this day, I have yet to find a single one.

What were the chances?

Did Spirit play a hand in that? Well, these kinds of "coincidences" happen to me a lot.

Donald Duck and a Lot of Luck

On the last day of primary school before the Easter holidays, our school held an Easter raffle for an enormous Donald Duck chocolate Easter egg. Raffle tickets were just twenty pence each and to most of the kids, that was nothing, but to me it was the world. All week long, raffle tickets sold. Each day, kids begged their parents for more money to buy more tickets.

But my mum could only afford one.

On the last day just before the school assembly, we were all in our classroom impatiently waiting for the clock to strike 9:00 am. Today someone would win the prized giant Easter egg. We talked about winning and how we would eat it whilst repeatedly checking the clock to see if the big finger had moved.

We all had our tickets laid out on the table. The teacher had written our names on the back of each ticket just in case we lost them during the week running up to Friday.

"I've got six tickets, how many have you got Bernard?" Ryan said.

Bernard, being partially sighted, counted out his tickets one by one onto the table, adjusting his very thick glasses after each one. When the last ticket hit the table, Bernard grinned, "I've got eight!"

Mathew raised his head from his folded arms and checked the clock on the wall. Nope it still wasn't nine o'clock yet.

"How many have you got David?" Mathew asked.

"One," I said.

"Just one? You've no chance of winning," he gloated.

BBBBRRRRIIIINGGGGGG...!!! The bell went and we all stood from our chairs.

Making our way along the corridor to the assembly hall, I felt a strange and overwhelming feeling of butterflies in my stomach. I couldn't explain it, but the feeling completely engulfed me. There are no words to describe it, in those few moments I just knew I was going to win that Easter egg.

In the assembly hall, all the kids sat cross-legged on the wooden floor as the headmistress addressed the school. The whole way through her speech the butterfly feeling stayed with me, growing stronger and stronger with each passing moment.

Again, that feeling of knowing I was going to win the Easter egg filled my stomach.

We were all desperate for the headmistress to finish talking and get on with the raffle. Whatever words of wisdom she was trying to leave us with were hopelessly overshadowed by the sight of the giant Easter egg sitting on the table. At last, she stopped talking and asked one of the teachers if they'd like to come forward and draw the winning raffle ticket.

Now she had the attention of every child in the hall.

One of the teachers stepped forward and reached into the box, with bated breath we fell silent.

Her hand came out of the box grasping just one ticket. We stretched our necks and moved our heads in various different positions trying to see what colour it was.

"It's a blue ticket. . . " She said loudly.

Mine was blue, my excitement rose and at this point my heart was almost beating out of my chest.

She unfolded the ticket slowly.

"The winner is . . . David Holt."

Everyone turned and looked at me. I tingled with excitement.

"David, can you stand up please and come to the front?"

Everyone clapped as I made the long walk to the front of the hall to receive my prize. As I stood there with the giant Donald Duck Easter egg in my arms, I felt like the king of the world.

The Haunted Guitar

Around the age of twelve, I found an old guitar up in the attic. What a great find.

I spent the day cleaning the years of dust and cobwebs off, polishing it up, and getting strings for it. I played with it all day. Before going to bed that night, I carefully placed it in the corner of my bedroom so that I could see it before I fell asleep.

Just as I was falling asleep, I heard the strings resonate, as if someone had given the guitar one quick strum.

My eyes flew open.

I could see the strings still vibrating. As the musical sound faded I looked around the room, but no one was there. We didn't have a cat or a dog at the time so an animal couldn't have made the sound. After a few moments, when the guitar remained silent and unmoving I convinced myself that what I had heard was just in my head. I had, after all, been playing with the guitar all day.

Warily, I closed my eyes and tried to sleep.

The second my eyes were shut the guitar strummed again, only quite a bit louder this time. I jumped and my eyes shot open.

Holding onto the duvet and with my heart thumping in my chest I muttered, "If it does it one more time . . ."

STRUM!

The guitar was definitely playing by itself.

I leapt out of bed, grabbed the guitar, and took it to my mother's room. Waking her from her sleep I shouted, "This guitar's just played by itself!"

"Well I don't want it in my room," was my mother's startled reply.

I picked the guitar up and set it out on the landing where it remained for the night. Mum and I spent the next hour or so sat wide-awake on the bed, waiting to see if the guitar out on the landing would serenade us one more time.

It didn't.

Not long after that night, the guitar ended up being put up for sale on a car boot sale. Neither Mum nor I wanted it in the house any more. The price was very low for such a nice guitar and at just eight pounds, it was quickly snatched up. It was a Hummingbird and the guy who bought it thought he'd got an excellent deal.

As the new owner walked happily away with his latest possession, my mother whispered, "You've got a bargain there, that one plays by itself."

❧

The following year was the first time I ever got a message from a medium.

At the grand old age of thirteen going on fourteen, I had been trusted with a set of keys to our house. "Keep these safe," Mum cautioned. And for a time I did.

But one day, I arrived home from school and discovered that I'd lost the keys. Despite looking absolutely everywhere for them, they were nowhere to be found.

That night, my mum had arranged to go to the local Spiritualist church with my two aunties and Nana.

I didn't want to go. I was worried that someone might find the lost keys and rob our house while we were gone.

Despite my protest, Mum persuaded me to go. My family was not particularly religious; they would go to the Spiritualist church every now and then, mainly when family members had passed.

As I sat in the old Spiritualist church for what seemed like an eternity, boredom seriously set in. And then the old lady on the platform picked out my mum.

"I have a grandmother here, can you take the name Hilda?"

That was Grandma Holt, my grandad's mum, the very lady we were all hoping to hear from. The medium spoke to each one of us, passing on various details and messages.

Then the medium pointed directly at me and said, "Keep drawing those faces."

I was stunned. The day before I had spent all afternoon drawing faces in pencil. Drawing, at that time, had become one of my hobbies.

She went on to say, "Spirit can bring lost things back to you, if you ask them."

Well, I was more than relieved to hear the medium say that. That night I lay in bed still filled with worry over my missing house keys, I asked the spirit world if they could bring them back to me.

The following morning I caught up with one of my close friends before school started. During our conversation about what we'd got up to last night and which TV shows we'd watched he said, "Hey D, you wanna see what I found last night? I'm keeping this, it's got a really cool keyring on it."

As he reached into his pocket I shouted, "THEY'RE MINE!"

Immediately he clamped both hands over his pocket to protect his find.

"No they ain't. . ." He frowned with confusion.

"It's a set of house keys with a green plastic keyring, it's got a real scorpion sealed inside it. They're mine!" He had a look of total disbelief on his face. I hadn't seen what he had in his pocket, but I just knew that they had to be my keys. He slowly pulled them out of his pocket and sure enough, there were my keys attached to the scorpion keyring. With a look of disappointment on his face, he slowly handed them over to me.

I was amazed by the message I'd been given at the Spiritualist church, and stunned that my keys really had been brought back to me.

This was the first time I had ever connected one of my strange "coincidences" with Spirit.

CHAPTER 3

Who . . . Me?

While I had experienced numerous interactions with the spirit world as a child, they diminished as I approached my teens. By the time I was about fifteen or so, my interactions with the spirit world were not nearly as frequent. Unusual things would still happen every now and then, particularly things involving synchronicity. But I didn't understand synchronicity yet, that was something I learned later.

As for having fewer interactions with the spirit world, I suspect the turbulence of a teenage mind compiled with changing hormones may have played a good part in that. Teenagers desperately search for some kind of identity and in doing so, they often fail to see themselves for who they really are. I was learning how to experience life and find my role in it.

Who was I?

What would I be?

What was I going to do?

As surprising as it may seem, the thought of being a medium had never entered my mind. I muddled on as best I could, the same as all teens the world over.

Additionally, I had been attending a born-again Christian church from the time I was fifteen. I asked many questions there, and at times, it seemed to make some of the leaders uncomfortable.

"If God created Earth, then why don't the rest of the planets have a purpose?"

"Why isn't there any mention of dinosaurs or Neanderthals in the Bible?"

And more importantly, "Did Adam and Eve have belly buttons?"

They wanted me to accept the things they believed without question. But questioning things is part of who I am.

I did mention in their presence wanting to go back to the Spiritualist church that I had attended several years previously.

They warned me that if I did, I would be walking into a pit of vipers. I was then subjected to various tales about mediums being involved in witchcraft and told that Spiritualists were followers of the devil.

Despite their efforts to frighten me into staying well away from the Spiritualist church, I still had an overwhelming feeling to go.

I finally rejected the judgement of the born-again Christians and left for good. I had just left my teens and my experiences with the spirit world were starting to return, becoming more and more frequent, just as they had been when I was a child. The overwhelming feeling I felt to visit the Spiritualist church was always accompanied by a strong butterfly sensation that I could feel in my stomach.

My mind was made up. I decided to go back to the same Spiritualist church I had once attended with my family. It was time for me to see if I could make sense of the experiences I was having.

I returned to the Spiritualist church on a Monday afternoon. From the moment I stepped inside, a calm and peaceful feeling surrounded me. I liked the idea of it being quiet and not very crowded.

On the wall hung pictures of previous church members who were now in the spirit world. At the front of the church was a rostrum and on it were vases filled with sweet smelling flowers. Gentle music played in the background as I quietly took a seat at the back of the church.

I sat and relaxed, waiting for the service to begin.

The chair lady, standing on the rostrum, welcomed everybody to the service before inviting us to join her in singing a hymn. Once the hymn ended, the medium taking the service was introduced. She was an older lady in her sixties.

The service began with the medium giving a short talk about the spirit world and how those in spirit were always with us and looking after us.

She then began to pass on spirit messages to members of the congregation. I sat back and listened, wondering if perhaps I would be lucky enough to get a message.

The medium had just finished giving a message to someone, and as she turned to take a sip of water from the table, a rush of butterflies filled my stomach.

"Can I come to the young man at the back?"

The dozen or so people present all turned around and looked at me.

I could feel the butterfly sensation getting stronger. Nervously I swallowed and gave a wobbly, "Yes."

At that point in my life, my stage fright was pretty paralyzing. Trying to speak in front of members of the public, even a small group, was a numbing experience.

"I have a lady here in the spirit world and she's coming through with two walking sticks, one in each hand."

It sounded like it could be my great-grandmother, Grandma Holt. The medium went on to describe her in more detail, mentioning various aspects about her life. Her description made it very evident that it was indeed the spirit of my great-grandmother.

"Spirit have been around you a lot lately young man. They're telling you not to worry, you are being helped and guided."

I found the message very comforting. I'd always felt close to my great-grandmother even though I'd only met her briefly as a child.

"Oh, I'm being told that you can talk to Spirit."

"Erm, okay." My heart started to beat a little faster as once again people turned to look at me.

"I can see you standing up here on this platform doing what I'm doing. You'll be working for Spirit."

You must be mad, was my first thought. There was no way in this world I was ever going to do that. I could barely speak up in front of a dozen people let alone stand on a stage and give messages from the spirit world.

The very thought of standing up there with all those eyes on me was enough to make me want to run a mile. I'd never be able to do that.

"Can I leave you with the love of this lady in spirit young man?"

"Yes," I replied. "Thank you."

I was delighted that my great-grandmother had come through to pass on her love and let me know that she was watching over me. But the part about me being a medium up there on the platform, I was still very unsure about.

Even though spirit people had made themselves present to me on numerous occasions throughout my childhood, I'd never thought of myself as a medium.

When the service was over, everyone gathered in the tea room next door.

Between biscuits being dunked and cakes being eaten, people discussed their messages and were having a good old chin wag about what they'd got up to over the weekend.

William, a long-standing member of the church, heard the message the medium had just given to me and asked if I'd thought of attending the weekly development circle at the church.

A development circle is a class held on a regular basis, usually once a week and is led by an experienced medium. The purpose of a development circle is to provide teaching and guidance on the subject of mediumship.

One Tuesday night, William drove me to the development circle meeting at the church. When we arrived, the church lay in darkness, the doors locked with nobody inside. William was as puzzled as I was. "I don't know why they're not meeting tonight, lad."

The next day we discovered that the circle had stopped running and wouldn't be starting up again for some time. While I still doubted that I would ever really be a medium, I was certainly intrigued with the idea of at least understanding my abilities.

Determined to help me find a circle, William introduced me to Jackie, a sincere and gentle medium who ran her own private development circle. William explained my situation to Jackie and asked if I could join her class.

"I'm not taking on any new mediums at the moment, William. My development circle is full," Jackie said.

I figured that was that.

But William persisted, "Jackie, just talk to the lad."

Jackie glanced over, gave me a warm smile, and pulled out a chair. "Come on then, let's have a chat."

So we sat and chatted. I don't quite know what she saw in me that day.

My connection to Spirit?

My potential to develop?

I really don't know. It didn't matter, whatever it was she accepted me into her development circle.

In fact, she did more than accept me. Jackie went out of her way to help me.

At that time, I had no car, and getting to Jackie's circle on a regular basis would have been difficult for me. Her commitment to me was so great that after working all day at the hospital, she would drive to my house, take me to her development circle, and drive me back home when we were done.

Jackie has to be one of the most sincere mediums I've ever met. Her development circle started me on the road to understanding who I was.

It was the re-awakening of all the spiritual abilities I'd had as a child and it would change my life forever.

CHAPTER 4

Jackie's Circle

When I first walked into the room of Jackie's development circle, I realized that I was very much outnumbered. All the members of the group were women of a certain age. And then there was me, a shy young man barely out of his teens.

At one point, there were one or two other men in the circle, but for the most part it was a group of women and I soon learned to be very comfortable working with that group.

They taught me how to interact with people, how to relax and just be myself.

I learned a lot about conversation, a lot about diets, and even more about women's problems!

The circle would meet weekly on a Wednesday night.

Each week Jackie started the circle with an opening prayer and then invited the spirit people to draw close. Jackie then gave the group various different exercises to do.

On my first night at the circle, Jackie led the group in a spiritual healing exercise.

One of us would remain seated in their chair while another stood behind them to give the healing. As this was my first night, I didn't know what to expect, so I decided to go second.

I remained seated in my chair while one of the women in the group came over and stood by my side.

"Just relax," she whispered.

A little apprehensive, I closed my eyes and tried to relax. She stood behind me and placed her hands on my shoulders.

The idea of this exercise was to try and tune into the person who was seated and get a sense of any ailments or emotional stresses they may have.

Healing would then be sent to those areas.

When this exercise first started, I was a little cynical. I couldn't really see the need for me to receive the healing. But, I couldn't see what harm it could do, so I went along with it.

As I sat there with my eyes closed allowing the woman to tune in to me, I really began to relax.

The longer I sat, the more relaxed I became.

Before long, I had completely forgotten where I was. It's very hard to describe, but in those moments all of life's troubles seemed to melt away. At that particular point in my life, I'd been suffering from a lot of stress and anxiety. To have such a feeling of deep peace and relaxation come over me was most unexpected.

There really had to be something to this. At one point I remember thinking, I don't want this to stop, I quite like it here.

When she was done, it was my turn.

Me?

Give spiritual healing to someone?

Still feeling a little amazed at what I'd just experienced, I stood behind the woman as she took her seat and listened to Jackie's instructions. Even though I felt less than confident in what I was about to do, Jackie's gentle manner was very reassuring.

"Place your hands on the shoulders of the person you're going to send healing to. I'd like you to try and tune in to the person you're healing, see if you can pick up on their health conditions or life situations where healing might be needed. You may pick up on physical ailments like back pains or headaches. Send healing thoughts to those areas."

After placing my hands on the shoulders of the woman in front of me, I closed my eyes and tried to tune in to her.

My focus quickly shifted from what I'd just experienced to what I was doing.

There was a notable change in the sensation around me compared to the feeling I'd experienced just moments before.

Once I relaxed and focused on tuning in to her, I could hardly believe it, but I actually felt the energy her body was giving off. I lifted my hands slightly above her shoulders but I could still feel it. Then, on either side of her head, the sensation was different still.

This was the most fascinating exercise I'd ever done. It was my first real experience at understanding the energy a human body emits and trying to do something really useful with my abilities.

It opened the door to many new experiences for me.

❧

The following week, we did a visualization exercise in the form of a guided meditation. We all sat comfortably with our eyes closed. Jackie instructed the group to take a nice deep breath, in through the nose and out through the mouth. After repeating the breathing exercise several times, all we had to do was relax and listen to the sound of her voice.

For the first few moments of the meditation, I really struggled to stop my mind wandering, jumping from one line of thought to another. Visions of what I'd done that day along with thoughts of what I had to do tomorrow kept popping in.

Fortunately for me, Jackie was well practiced in leading a group meditation. She spoke softly and guided our thoughts to let go of all the activities and stresses of the day. As I listened to her voice, my mind began to settle and become still.

"I'd like you to visualize a castle in your mind's eye as clearly and in as much detail as you possibly can. Visualizing the green grass underneath your feet as you walk towards the entrance."

Jackie spoke slowly, allowing enough time for the vision to develop in our minds.

"Inside the castle is a table. What does it look like? How big is it? What colour?"

The more I relaxed and the more I listened to Jackie's voice the clearer the vision became.

The meditation continued.

"On the table is a shiny red apple . . . see it clearly. Sitting alongside the apple is a sharp and gleaming knife. I'd like you to pick up the knife and slice the apple in two. Take a good look at the inside of the apple. See the glistening white flesh. Now count the apple pips inside. How many are there?"

Soon Jackie had us gently return to a normal waking state. This was my first go at meditation.

Although I'd enjoyed this mental exercise, I couldn't understand how meditating and visualizing a castle in my mind was going to help me communicate with the spirit world.

But visions and images play a big part in spirit communication, all I had to do was be patient and allow Spirit to lead the way.

CHAPTER 5

Spiritual Language

Practice makes perfect. The more time you spend with someone, the better you get to know them. You know their thoughts, their feelings, what you can expect of them, and what you can't. Over time, your bond gets stronger, you can contact them at any time and talking to that person becomes as easy as breathing.

For me, talking to Spirit is no different.

Jackie's weekly circle rekindled that relationship I'd had with Spirit since childhood. It was the ideal place for my mediumistic abilities to reopen, resurface, and to practice, practice, practice my communication skills.

Talking to Spirit is easy; you simply talk just as you would to anyone else. There is no need of any unusual rituals or special words that must be used. But learning how to receive messages from individual spirit people is different.

Not all spirit people communicate in the same way. Just as each person in this world is unique and individual in their nature, the same can be said for people in the spirit world.

Some are bold and confident, well-spoken and clear. Others are shy and quiet and getting a conversation out of them can be difficult. Some spirit people are well practiced in coming through, while others are attempting it for the very first time.

This is where the spiritual language of mediumship comes in. It is a language of thoughts and feelings, images and pictures.

The development circle was the one night of each week I specifically dedicated to spending time with Spirit and developing my spiritual language skills.

Sitting in the circle and inviting spirit people to come forward was always (and still is) a fascinating experience for me. There is a very distinctive feeling that comes when spirit people are present.

The sensation feels like hundreds of butterflies in my stomach, or solar plexus to be more precise.

The moment this feeling comes, I know the spirit world is ready to communicate. It's like their way of saying, "We're here."

When spirit people talk to me, I hear their voices in two very distinctive ways, sometimes internally and sometimes externally.

An internal spirit voice (*clairaudience*) comes in the form of an amplified thought inside my mind. It is much louder than my own thoughts and is accompanied by an overwhelming feeling to speak the words aloud.

External spirit voices are a little harder to describe. It's like a gentle whisper in my ear. Often quietly spoken but on some occasions can be just as loud as a normal voice. Rather like a radio receiving a broadcast that is slightly out of tune, some words are faint and hard to detect whilst other words come through crisp, loud and clear.

In order to help develop and focus our minds when receiving thought flows and spirit voices, Jackie had a clever little exercise up her sleeve.

We would sit with our eyes closed and listen carefully as a piece of classical music played. We had to choose one instrument from the symphony and follow it all the way through the entire piece, whilst filtering out all the other instruments.

This helped me to develop my hearing ability so that I could tune out all other sounds but that of the spirit I was communicating with.

To this day, I still find myself listening to music in the car and at the end of the song realize that I haven't actually heard any of the words. I'd just been following one of the instruments. I guess some old habits die hard, or don't die at all.

Clairvoyance is a word that is used very loosely these days. Most people are no longer aware of its true meaning or what it involves.

It is a French word that translates as "clear seeing." This is the ability to see into the spirit world and receive images and pictures (visions) from the other side.

Spirit people often communicate using this form of mediumship.

Whether I'm giving a public demonstration of mediumship or conducting a private reading I invariably receive clairvoyant images from the spirit world.

These images are so vivid I not only see them in my mind's eye, but also externally, they can appear just as real as any other object in the room.

During a clairvoyant vision, I can be shown anything from the inside of a person's home to the personal items that were placed in the coffin of a loved one.

I see names written up in front of me along with a whole host of other things. Faces and photographs, birthday cakes and flowers. If it is meaningful to the recipient or important to the message, Spirit will find a way of impressing the vision on my mind. On occasion, I have felt compelled to draw what I have seen for the sitter to keep and compare to the original item. Things like medals, jewellery, and even old postage stamps.

When I pass on messages from spirit people, I can feel their presence around me; this ability is known as *clairsentience*.

I am able to feel if they are male or female, older or younger, and as the communication progresses I am quickly made aware of a lot more.

I know how they died and how they felt at the point of their transition. Be it old age or a heart attack, illness or suicide, if a spirit person can convey that sensation to me I will feel it.

I can sense their character, experience their memories, and feel their emotions as the desire to come through and connect with their loved ones gets stronger.

With such strong feelings come a lot of emotions, and at times they can be very powerful. There have been occasions when I have been brought to tears through the emotions that are expressed during a reading.

There is no training on how to deal with such sensations. Interpreting those feelings and emotions only comes with time and experience.

Jackie had a fun and lighthearted way of developing our sensing abilities.

One Wednesday night, Jackie started the circle by producing a blind fold and asking for a volunteer. For a moment I wondered what on earth she had planned on doing whilst we were blindfolded.

My curiosity got the better of me but before I could speak, one of the middle-aged ladies in the circle stood up and said, "I'll do it Jackie, it's been a while since anyone blindfolded me!" That statement received much chuckling and laughter from the rest of us.

We each took it in turn to be the one sat in the hot seat wearing the blindfold. When it was my turn, I sat there, my chair facing the wall and my back to the rest of the group.

Jackie then silently instructed another member of the circle to stand ten feet behind me.

"Okay David, they're starting to walk towards you."

The aim of this exercise was to sense when the person was getting close and say, "Stop, I can feel you."

Once we had done that, we then had to tune into the person and describe them. Male or female, tall or short. We would then push ourselves further and describe the feelings that we could pick up from them. If their day had been busy and stressful, or calm and relaxing. What they had eaten for breakfast and what sort of things they'd got up to that day.

All throughout the exercise, they remained silent so as not to give away their identity to the blindfolded medium. They would only nod or shake their head to Jackie to indicate how accurate our statements were.

This exercise was great fun at times and was a wonderful way to practice our clairsentient abilities in a playful and relaxed manner. The more relaxed we were the better it got, but Jackie had ways of pushing our abilities even further.

Sometimes she would have three or four people standing behind us and we wouldn't know. On the odd occasion, Jackie would even have us sitting there trying to tune into the person behind us without there being anyone there at all! It was a brilliant technique to keep us on our toes.

At the end of each circle, we would practice our mediumship by giving messages to each other. This was the best way of bringing together all the mediumistic skills we had been developing.

Hearing spirit voices, seeing clairvoyant images, interpreting feelings, and putting them all together to deliver an accurate message from the spirit world may seem like a daunting and complicated process.

However, the more you speak the spiritual language of mediumship, the more fluent you become. I often liken this to a learner trying to drive a car for the first time. First you have to start the engine, press the clutch, and select the correct gear. Lift the clutch, press the accelerator, and set off without stalling.

At the same time, you have to steer the vehicle, signal accordingly, adhere to the speed limit, follow road signs, watch for pedestrians and other motorists, and keep gearing up and down, all while trying to find where you are going!

To anyone getting behind the wheel of a car for the very first time, this seems like an almost impossible task. But to any experienced driver who has been on the road a few years, it's second nature.

With practice and experience, you bring all those different elements together without really having to think about it.

I had been talking to Spirit ever since I was a child, I simply didn't recognize it for what it was back then.

Like anyone who can speak another language, the more time you spend speaking it, the more it becomes a part of you.

There have been periods when I have spent so much time communicating with the spirit world that I've forgotten my own physical language!

Just a few years ago, I went through a most unusual phase. It was at a time when I was so busy with mediumship it was pretty much all I did, seven days a week.

During this phase there were numerous times when I would ask my wife what our lunch plans were. And when I got no reply I would rather abruptly ask her again, followed with the tag line, "Is there a reason you're ignoring me?"

When my wife explained that I hadn't spoken a word I was puzzled. I had indeed spoken the words, but the problem was I'd only done it in my mind. I was thinking my words but wasn't vocalizing them, I only thought that I had.

"I'm not a mind reader you know, that's your job," my wife would say.

It was such a strange thing that was happening to me and just as I thought I had started to move on from it, the very opposite began to happen, sometimes with disastrous results.

One afternoon, my wife and I were seated at a table in a restaurant. It was a small break in the middle of a very busy day where we could both just sit down and relax. Moments after we'd placed our order, a rather obnoxious woman walked in and sat at a table close by.

As I sat there in an almost daydream like state, thoughts of what I'd like to say to that woman filled my mind. And then, "Honey, you know you just said that out loud, right?"

"Erm..did I?"

I had no idea that I had actually spoken my thoughts out loud.

Needless to say, speaking your mind is not always recommended, especially in a public place.

CHAPTER 6

Spirit Guides

In the world of mediums and Spiritualists, you are sure to come across the subject of spirit guides. But what are they? And who are they?

Traditionally, spirit guides are seen as spirit mediators between this world and the next. It is believed that each medium is appointed a spirit guide who will make themselves known to the medium during the course of their development.

There are different views on what the role of the spirit guide actually is. Some believe it is the guide who brings through the spirit people, and conveys their messages to the medium. Others believe the guide to be like a spiritual helper who assists the medium on their spiritual journey and aids them in passing on messages from the spirit world.

Over the years, my experience with delivering spirit messages and spending the vast majority of my time with Spirit has changed my views on guides.

I do believe strongly that there are spirit influences on the other side who come to help and guide us at certain times in our lives. Their presence and guidance usually comes to us exactly when it is needed.

In my early days, I was aware of my guide each and every time I worked with Spirit. But as my experience with mediumship grew, I became less aware of a guide and more aware of Spirit. Now, whenever I'm delivering spirit messages, I am only aware of the spirit person who wishes to communicate, not the presence of any particular guide.

Early in my development, I'd heard so many different things about spirit guides I didn't know what to make of them. But after hearing so much about them, I was quite looking forward to finding out who my spirit guide was, and I didn't have to wait long.

One Wednesday, during her development circle, Jackie held a group meditation, which would introduce us to our spirit guides. I was intrigued and excited at what might happen. During this deep and relaxing meditation, Jackie instructed us to ask our guides to step forward and introduce themselves.

When the group came back to our normal waking state, Jackie asked each of us in turn to describe what we had seen and the guide who had come forward in our vision.

Each person described their experience giving wonderful accounts of spiritual places and historical figures; Egyptian kings, wise Buddhist monks, Native American chiefs, and all kinds of spiritual beings.

As I sat listening to the group give their accounts of the meditation, I wondered what I had done wrong.

I didn't see or experience any of that.

All I saw was my great grandmother, Grandma Holt. The same grandma who had come through to me at the Spiritualist church a few weeks before. She was simply standing and smiling at me, looking just as I'd remembered her from my childhood.

It was almost my turn to speak, but I felt very reluctant to mention what I had seen. I wondered if I should just make something up to fit in with the rest of the group, a Roman emperor, or wise philosopher perhaps.

"David, what did you see?" Jackie gently asked, giving me no time to come up with a more fascinating guide.

"Erm, well I followed your guidance but all I saw was my great-grandma."

"That's wonderful." Jackie said. "She's looking after you and guiding you at the moment." Jackie turned to the next person, then looked back at me and added, "She'll likely help you when you begin working on the platform."

With the exception of the working on platform reference, I felt pretty good about Grandma Holt being my guide. It was nice to have someone that close and special guiding me as I continued my journey of development.

CHAPTER 7

My First Public Appearance

When the spirit world decides it is time for you to work for them, they will present you with the opportunity to do so.

They will make sure that you are in the right place, at the right time.

Usually, this happens when you are least expecting it.

Approximately seven weeks after joining Jackie's development group, I attended a Thursday night service at the Spiritualist church.

Both Jackie and her mother were there, and I stood chatting with them in the tea room before the service began.

Jackie had just popped a chocolate snowball into her mouth when a rather anxious member of the church committee approached her.

"Jackie, I'm chairing tonight and the medium has just rung up and cancelled. Can you do the service for us please?"

To the relief of the chairperson Jackie smiled and agreed to take the service. As she finished off her chocolate snowball, I teased, "Now you didn't see that coming, did you?"

With a cheeky grin on her face, Jackie narrowed her eyes and said, "I don't know what you're laughing at lad, you're coming up with me!"

Gulp! For a moment, I didn't know what to say, I couldn't tell if she were joking or not.

The chairperson offered Jackie the use of the medium's room, a small room located at the back of the church where mediums could go and sit quietly with Spirit to gather their thoughts before a service.

Jackie finished her drink and made her way to the medium's room next door.

I sat in the congregation next to Jackie's mother.

Having a joke and a little banter with Jackie was quite common, but for some reason the comment about me going up on the platform with her wouldn't leave my thoughts. I also became aware of that butterfly feeling, the same feeling I got each week at the circle when we invited Spirit to come forward.

"You don't think she's being serious do you? About me going on the platform?"

Jackie's mother looked at me, "No, she's only kidding."

Phew! I thought. After all, I'd only been in the circle a little less than two months. Whenever I saw guest mediums demonstrating at the church, they always spoke about how many years they had spent developing before working on the platform.

Why worry? I banished my concern and settled in my seat.

I quite looked forward to seeing my circle leader demonstrating on the platform. I wondered if I could tune into Jackie whilst she worked to see if I could pick up the same things she was getting.

More and more people arrived and the seats in the church filled quickly. It was now 7:30 pm and time for the service to start. Jackie came out of the medium's room at the back of the church and walked down the aisle toward the platform at the front.

As she approached the row that we were sitting in, she stopped. "Well, come on then. I said you were coming up with me."

Stunned, I stared at her, then looked desperately at her mother hoping for some reassurance that Jackie was joking. Even Jackie's mother seemed unsure.

"Come on, you'll be all right."

Numbly, I rose from my seat and followed her up to the platform. My heart started to beat faster and faster, and I could feel myself shaking with nerves. With each step I took, my legs felt like jelly.

To say I was nervous was an understatement.

I took my seat on the platform and for the first time looked out at the congregation. Wow, I'd never seen the church from this angle before. What a daunting sight, all those people looking at me so expectantly. It felt nothing like sitting in the comfort of the development circle.

I remembered what a visiting medium once said before taking the service, "If a medium doesn't feel nervous before they give a demonstration then they aren't going to be much good."

Well, if nervousness indicates good mediumship, Bolton Spiritualist Church was about to witness the greatest medium who ever lived. I tried taking deep breaths to settle myself before my nerves spiralled out of control. For a moment, I thought it was going to be impossible to sense the spirit world in this state. Please let this work, I thought.

The chairperson introduced us both as the mediums for the night, then everyone sang a hymn. During the hymn, Jackie reassured me that I would be okay, explaining that she would go first and give messages, and if I felt that I had something during the service I could stand up and give it a try.

But what if it didn't work?

What if I got everything wrong?

And what if nobody accepted my messages?

The hymn ended, time for the demonstration of mediumship to begin. Jackie started with an opening prayer then delivered spirit messages to members of the congregation.

I sat there with my eyes closed trying to forget that all those people were out there looking at me. I begged the spirit world to come forward. Suddenly I became aware of Grandma Holt. I held onto her presence like a lifeline. Then I heard Jackie's voice, "David, would you like to stand up and give a message?" My eyes popped open.

"I'm not sure, I don't think I've got anything."

"Yes you have, I can see you've got someone with you, stand up and have a go. I'll help you."

I nervously stood and walked to the centre of the platform. I felt drawn to a woman sitting close to the front. The butterfly feeling that indicated the presence of Spirit radiated from my stomach.

"I can see your mum with you in spirit. She's holding a bunch of yellow chrysanthemums."

I didn't even know what chrysanthemums were, but the woman's face lit up as she nodded and smiled.

"She knows you want to move house, you're in a flat at the moment and you don't like it."

"That's right."

"She heard you asking her for help the other day whilst putting her photos into an album."

Everything I said, the woman acknowledged as correct. She had tears in her eyes and a big smile on her face.

Phew! I'd done it.

I'd just given my very first public message, it was short and sweet but well received and accepted with a smile and a thank you.

I returned to my seat on the platform with the most amazing feeling inside me. I felt a lightness in my chest like a weight had been lifted.

"Well done, David. I told you you'd be all right."

Again, I sat there with my eyes closed waiting for the next connection to come through. Before long, I felt the spirit of a gentleman around me. Again, Jackie asked me if I'd like to have another go at giving a message.

"Yes. I think I've got a gentleman with me who wants to come through," I said.

I stood at the front of the platform, this time Jackie stepped back and sat down. It may have only been a couple of steps further away, but for me it felt like my safety net had disappeared. To add a little more pressure, it was now 8:25 pm, which meant that this message was going to be the last one of the night.

Spirit drew me to a man at the back of the church.

"Can I come to you sir?"

"Er, yes okay."

Immediately Spirit gave me a vision of a car being repaired.

"You have a gentleman with you in spirit, and he's watched you repairing your car recently."

The man stared at me blankly. "No, I didn't fix my car."

Ugh! My heart sank and my nerves started to creep back. I was wrong. How could Spirit be wrong? I followed Jackie's instruction and asked the spirit world to give me more information, but the same vision came back, only more clearly this time.

"I'm still being shown that this has something to do with a car being repaired, and it happened today."

Again, the man shook his head, frowning, "No, I don't think this is for me."

Ugh . . . I felt like I'd just had the wind knocked out of me. The church fell silent and I could almost feel all those eyes on me. In my mind, I begged the spirit world to give me something else, something different, anything as long as it was right!

It must only have been seconds but it felt like an eternity waiting for Spirit to give me another piece of information. As I stood there, a woman with a puzzled look on her face gave the man a dig in the ribs, then she muttered something to him. With a sudden look of realization on his face, he said, "Well, I had to change one of the back tires on my wife's car this afternoon, does that mean anything?"

"Ohhhhh..." The entire congregation groaned and then burst into laughter.

I almost collapsed in relief.

The chairperson called time and the service ended.

Before we left the platform, Jackie gave me a big hug and said, "Well done, David, you've made me very proud tonight."

The moment I stepped off the platform a woman in the congregation approached me and asked if I did private readings.

Private readings?

Me?

I was really taken back. I explained that I was only a beginner and nowhere near ready for that.

I felt a glowing feeling of joy, excitement, and relief inside me all mixed together. Only when we got back in the tea room did I remember the message I'd been given that Monday afternoon a few months ago. What the old lady had said to me from the very same platform had just come true. Maybe the spirit world did have plans for me after all.

∽∾

Anybody who walks out onto a stage and stands in front of a crowd has to have a certain amount of belief in what they are about to do. Singers practice constantly to perfect their voice and rehearse their songs frequently until they know each one of them off by heart. When it comes to their performance, they know exactly which songs they are going to sing and in what order they're going to sing them.

I know of actors who read their scripts over two hundred and fifty times before filming begins just to make sure they are completely familiar with the lines they are going to deliver.

Mediumship has to be one of the few things that is demonstrated live without there being any possibility of a rehearsal. Sure, you can practice your abilities to connect with the other side in a circle, but what happens when you step out there to demonstrate mediumship is in the hands of the spirit world.

Spirit will sometimes have an agenda for an evening of mediumship that is completely different to our own. They decide what messages come through and which spirit people are in the plan of things for that evening, not the medium.

After my first evening on the platform with Jackie, the spirit world began to provide me with many more opportunities to work for them. Every now and then Jackie would phone me to ask if I'd like to join her on platform at her next demonstration, and I usually accepted her invitation.

Within a couple of years Bolton Spiritualist Church booked me to do my first Sunday service, and not long after that other Spiritualist churches started to book me as well.

My sensitivity to Spirit really opened up at this stage and I could feel their presence around me night and day. I really enjoy the presence of Spirit, so much so that in my eyes there was no such thing as spending too much time with them.

I would never turn down a Spiritualist church that wanted my service and the thought of cancelling one never crossed my mind. I would have to be dead before I'd cancel and even then I'd probably have still turned up and done it! No two evenings are ever the same. It doesn't matter how many times I step out onto that platform, each night is always a new experience for me; no rehearsal and nothing to fall back on, just my trust in Spirit and my ability to hear them.

❧

One night I was taking a Sunday service at a Spiritualist church in Horwich. I particularly enjoyed working in this church, partly due to its old-fashioned interior and interesting Spiritualist paraphernalia that hang from its walls. And partly because you were almost guaranteed a perfectly made cup of tea and a fantastic selection of cakes before and after the service.

This night people packed the church from front to back and I could feel the presence of Spirit strongly in the room. When I began the service, the spirit world communicated immediately, there was no hesitation from those on the other side. The messages came through with ease, thick and fast, one after the other.

Before I knew it, I was called to time and the service was over.

I came off the platform to a queue of people thanking me for the service and requesting private readings. When the connection with the spirit world is this strong, the mediumship is almost effortless. You certainly don't leave the platform feeling drained, it is quite the opposite. You are glowing with energy.

When my wife and I got home after the service, the strong feeling of Spirit that I'd felt on the platform had followed us home. It was so strong that we were both filled with energy and neither one of us could sleep.

Finally, it started to fade away and we could both get some rest.

The following night I had another Spiritualist church service. After what we'd experienced at Horwich church the night before we were both quite looking forward to it.

We pulled up in the car outside the church, and as my wife put on the handbrake I got a very strange feeling in my stomach.

"You okay hun? Do you wanna go straight inside or do you want a minute?"

"I don't want to go inside at all. Something doesn't feel right."

I couldn't really explain how I felt, I just had a feeling that I didn't want to walk through those doors. But, I was booked to do the service and cancelling is something I never do. Despite the strange feeling, we both made our way inside.

The church members were polite and friendly and the first thing they did was offer us both a cup of tea. We took a seat in the annex, and as they dashed off to make the tea the strange feeling I had got worse. For the life of me, I couldn't put my finger on what was wrong.

A lady came back with two cups of tea. "There you go, help yourself to sugar and milk. Are you both okay?"

"Yes, we're fine thank you." I replied. But my response couldn't have been further from the truth. I sat there slowly stirring my tea wondering why on earth I felt so despondent.

"How are you feeling now, Honey?" my wife asked.

"I feel like I just want to go home."

"Yeah, me too." To my surprise my wife was also experiencing this same strange sensation.

There was nothing I could do, it was almost time for the service. The church president came over, shook my hand and explained that he would be chairing for me that evening. My wife gave me a hug to reassure me that I'd be okay, and as she did I whispered in her ear, "I still wanna go home."

The president led me into the church and I made my way up the steps onto the platform. As we sang our way through the hymns I desperately tried to shake the feeling off me.

I looked out at the congregation as they sang. It should have felt like any other church service, like I'd done dozens of times before.

But it didn't.

I was there, the congregation was there, and everything appeared to be as it should. But there was one important thing missing . . .

. . .Spirit!

I couldn't feel a single thing.

This was the first time I'd ever felt like this and I wasn't comfortable with it at all. The hymns were over and the president began to address the congregation.

"Tonight's medium is David Holt, he's a young medium from Bolton with a reputation for giving very accurate and detailed messages. It's a pleasure to have him here, so please give him a warm welcome. I'm sure we're going to have a brilliant service. David, may I hand the service over to you?"

Well after that introduction, you can imagine what kind of expectation the congregation had. Their smiling faces looked back at me waiting for these accurate and detailed messages to come through. I still couldn't feel anything so I decided to give them a brief talk about the way I receive messages as a medium. I was hoping that whilst giving my little talk something would start to happen and I'd be back to my normal self.

In my mind, I sent out a thought to the other side, *"Okay Spirit, if ever there was a time for you to come through and start giving messages, it's now!"*

Any minute now, I thought . . . but still . . . nothing!

I had only one option. Be honest, and tell them that nothing was coming through.

So I did.

The problem was the congregation didn't seem to believe me, they all thought I was joking and burst out laughing. I had to explain that I really wasn't joking and that I could go no further with the service.

I sat down in my chair on the platform, worried about what the president might say, as this was my first service at the church. But, I needn't have worried. When I looked over at him, he was so engrossed in a bidding war on E-bay that he hadn't even noticed the service had come to an abrupt finish.

A few awkward moments passed as we all sat there in silence and he continued to punch in numbers on his laptop trying to win the bid.

By now, the silence must have grabbed his attention. He looked up at the congregation, and then across at me.

There was a look of total confusion on his face; it was obvious that he was not aware of what had just happened. Flummoxed by the silence and the sight of me sitting down, he leapt to his feet, grabbed hold of a hymn book and said, "May we all join in singing the final hymn?"

As we all sang the hymn, he kept looking at his watch and then back at me trying to make sense of the situation. After he invited me to say the closing prayer, the service was finally over.

I couldn't wait to get out of there and get back in the car. I made my way off the platform as quickly as I could, but as I came down the steps both the president and the booking secretary were waiting for me. I wondered what on earth they were going to say.

"Thank you David, we'll give you a call soon and book you for another service."

What? I was quite surprised at that response. I thought perhaps the booking secretary had felt sorry for me and wanted to give me another chance.

The lesson I took from that experience was that no matter what our expectations are of the spirit world, they certainly don't have to meet them.

Quite often as Spiritualists, we take it for granted that the spirit world is going to show up each week at our set time and at our set place.

The unseen world is not at our beck and call.

As mediums, we make ourselves available to the spirit world to pass on any messages that may need to be delivered. If there are no messages in the spiritual plan of things on that occasion, there is nothing we can do to change that.

CHAPTER 8

Psychic or Medium?

P art of the reason for this first book is to help people understand exactly what a medium is, what a medium can do, and what a medium cannot do.

As a medium, I find that people are often confused with the difference between mediums, psychics, fortunetellers, card-readers, etc.

What exactly is the difference between a psychic and a medium? Or are they just the same?

The word psychic stems from the Greek word *psychikos* which means "of the mind" the human mind (or psyche) to be precise.

It has long been believed that psychic phenomena are produced by the human mind and not associated with spirits or the spirit world. However, just where exactly the line is drawn between what is deemed psychic and what is mediumistic isn't always clear.

Psychics have the ability to pick up information without using the five known senses. This is known as Extra Sensory Perception, (ESP).

Psychic ability covers a wide variety of phenomena ranging from mental telepathy (mind reading) to remote viewing, dowsing, metal bending, and even telekinesis, which is the ability to move objects with the mind.

By merely touching or focusing on an object, psychics are able to glean information about a person, a place, or an event. Commonly known as psychometry, this ability has been used to find missing people and has even played a part in solving crimes such as murders.

Psychics and the phenomena they produce tend not to focus on the afterlife or communicating with spirit people.

Psychics pick up information from this world and can tune into the living, whereas mediums are able to tune into the next world and communicate with the dead, or spirit people.

Although it is true that the majority of psychic phenomena does not provide evidence of an afterlife, it is impossible to say with any degree of certainty that Spirit is not involved in some way.

Nowadays, the majority of psychics come in the form of tarot card readers, crystal ball gazers, and palm readers.

People consult psychics over personal matters, decisions, and situations regarding the past, present, and of course, the future.

As fascinating and as insightful as these forms of divination can be, their focus is purely on the sitter's life situations. It does not involve communicating with spirit people.

This is where I come in.

As a medium, I am able to expand my mind beyond the vibrations of this world and into the next. It is in this state that I communicate with the conscious minds of those who have died and crossed over.

I get a glimpse into their world, see their faces, hear their voices, feel their presence, and pass on their messages.

When we pass away, it is our consciousness that survives death and makes the transition to the spirit world. It is the living consciousness of discarnate spirit people that I, as a medium, am communicating with whenever I deliver spirit messages.

When I conduct a reading for someone, my purpose is to speak on behalf of the spirit person who wishes to come through. Mediumship provides an opportunity for spirit people to convey their messages and show their loved ones that they are still with them. During this communication, evidential statements and personal messages are passed on to the sitter, which proves beyond all doubt that their loved ones are alive and well in the spirit world. Mediumship brings great comfort to the bereaved, helps to heal grief, and reunites the recipient of the message with their loved one on the other side.

It's a common misconception that mediums can call up the dead. In fact, nothing could be further from the truth. No medium has the power to demand the presence of any particular spirit person.

It is actually the dead, or spirit people, who call on the medium to communicate. I've had people approach me and say, "You're disturbing the dead!" and "The dead should be left to rest." It is quite evident those people have no understanding of mediumship or the spirit communication process. I've dedicated my entire life to passing on messages on behalf of the spirit world and believe me, if they don't want to be contacted, there is nothing a medium can do to make them speak.

Over the years, I have been asked to contact many famous people such as Albert Einstein, John Wayne, Elvis Presley, and numerous other celebrities. And, on just one occasion, I was asked to contact Adolf Hitler.

I know for sure that my uncle David, whom I was named after, would have given anything for me to make contact with The King. He had all of his albums, knew all of his songs, and if ever The King's talent was in dispute, my uncle would leap to his defense and say, "Excuse me, there's nowt wrong wit King."

However, spirit communication doesn't work that way. I cannot make contact with a famous person on request, not unless you have some sort of personal relationship with that individual.

If, however I were asked to hold a sitting for one of John Wayne's relatives, there would, of course, be a very real chance that The Duke would come through. They have a personal relationship and an emotional bond with their relative in spirit. And the same must be said for anyone wishing to make contact with someone in the spirit world.

But, even if this is so, contact with the other side is not always a certainty.

There have been occasions when I have sat with a client to make contact with the spirit world, only to find there's no answer from the other side.

There are a number of reasons why this can happen. It could be that you simply don't need a message at that time or that you aren't ready to hear what they have to say.

Spirit people know when we are ready to accept their messages even if we think we are ready to receive them now. They have our best interests in mind.

There has to be a need for the mediumship to take place and a reason for the spirit person to come through in order for the process to work.

Just like our relatives in this world, there are days when we get a phone call from them and they can talk for hours. And there are times when we don't hear from them at all. It doesn't necessarily mean that there is anything wrong. In fact quite the opposite.

In most cases, no news is good news.

They'll call when they need to. In the same way, our spirit friends and relatives will come through as and when they are ready.

Some people believe that you have to wait a certain amount of time after a loved one has passed before they can be contacted. I've heard people say you must wait six months, or even twelve months before they can come through. In my experience, this is completely untrue.

There is no set amount of time that has to pass before a spirit person can come through. It doesn't matter if they've been gone twenty years or just twenty minutes. If they need to, they will find a way to come through to us.

Before you decide to have a reading with either a psychic or a medium, you should always ask yourself *why* you want to see them. Once you know the answer to this question then you will know which one of them is best suited to your needs. If indeed, you need to see one at all.

If you are looking for an insight into your current life or are hoping for a glimpse into what your future may hold, then a reading with a psychic would be the way to go.

However, if you wish to connect with a loved one who has passed away, then a sitting with a medium is what you need.

There is a world of difference between communicating with spirit people and telling someone their fortune. While mediums can sometimes provide insight into current situations and even future events, this is not the reason to consult one.

If you have lost someone dear to you, be sure you have taken time to grieve and heal before consulting a medium. It is always best to approach a reading with a calm and collected mind, not a grief-stricken and desperate one. When you feel you are ready for a reading with a medium, finding a good one is essential, but not always easy. Generally word of mouth is the best way.

If you are completely new to the experience, having a family member or friend accompany you during your reading can also be a good idea.

Once you have received that contact from a loved one in spirit, it is important to use the experience as a way of moving forward, secure in the knowledge that they're still around you.

CHAPTER 9

Red Wine and Pizza

Now, when someone has lost a loved one and there is a real need for mediumship to take place, it is then that the most amazing communications come through from the other side. The messages the spirit people give in order to prove to their loved ones that they are still alive can be breathtaking.

Reuniting families with their loved ones in spirit, seeing grief healed, and tears of joy are the motivations behind everything I do.

Cathy, a lovely lady in her late sixties, had arranged for a private reading to take place at her home. I walked through the front door and into the living room. She offered me a seat and cup of tea. I sat back on the sofa and whilst listening to the sounds of the kettle boiling and spoons clinking in the next room, I became aware of the spirit of a young woman watching me. Her presence was strong and she felt very eager to connect with us.

Cathy explained that she had never done anything like this before and didn't know what to expect.

She sat back in the chair as I put her at ease and explained that nothing spooky or frightening would happen.

The spirit of the young woman began to communicate almost immediately.

"I can feel the spirit of a young woman with you. She's very close to you. She's thirty-eight years old and she's telling me that she passed away with breast cancer."

"That's my daughter! Sarah!" Cathy's eyes grew wide with excitement and emotion.

"She's a beautiful looking woman with green eyes and long dark hair and wants you to know that she is with you and her father all the time."

Cathy smiled.

"She's showing me a map of South Africa."

"That's where her father is working right now!"

Sarah's voice became much clearer and the communication with her got faster and faster.

"She wants you to tell Dad that she loves him. She knows that you have kept a lock of her hair; it's in a silver locket that you keep on top of the dresser in the bedroom. And she wants you to know that in the spirit world she's got all of her long dark hair back."

Before her passing, Sarah had lost most of her hair due to the cancer treatment. Her mother was delighted to hear that Sarah now resembled her former self before the illness had taken hold.

As the reading progressed, Sarah continued to provide me with many more details about the afterlife, including the names of family members she'd never met in this world, but had now connected with in the spirit world. She also listed a number of birthday gifts that she had received from her parents along with details about various different holidays they had shared.

Specific details like these that a spirit person provides are significant only to the recipient of the message.

As such, it is these details that prove beyond all doubt that the medium is in communication with their loved one.

Just as the reading seemed to be reaching an end the atmosphere in the room completely changed, and we were both filled with a powerful feeling of emotion.

I was then shown a glimpse of where Sarah was on the other side. It was beautiful, peaceful, and calm. And yet at the same time, it was quite a familiar and recognizable place.

"I can see your daughter, she's sitting outside on a patio, it looks like Spain and it's a warm sunny day. She's sitting at a table with a glass of red wine and eating a big slice of pizza."

As soon as I'd described what I'd seen the vision faded and the message was complete.

Cathy, wiping her eyes, slowly got up from her chair and walked across the living room to a set of wooden drawers, pulled open the top drawer and removed an envelope.

"I want you to read this, David," Cathy said as she handed it to me.

I gently opened the envelope and removed a hand-written letter from inside. Sarah had written this letter to her mother whilst she was in hospital in the last few days of her life. She had sealed it and asked her mother only to open it after her passing.

As I read each heart-felt word, I could feel emotion building inside my chest. These were the last written words of a dying woman to her mother. I felt so honored to be reading such a personal and special letter, a letter filled with so much meaning and emotion behind every single word.

Thank you for being the best mum a girl could ever wish for. For your big squeeze hugs and your make all-better kisses. For teaching me to walk and how to tie my laces. I cherish every memory of every moment we've ever spent together. You were there for my first steps and you're here for my last.

I couldn't ask for a better mum to be at my side.

By the time I reached the bottom of the page I had a painful lump in my throat and was fighting back my tears. I turned the page over and read the last paragraph.

Mum, I know that my time in this world is coming to an end, I want you to know that I have made peace with that and have come to terms with my illness. I don't know if I believe in God, but if there is such a thing as heaven you will find me there, sat out doors, with the sun shining on my face, drinking a large glass of red wine and eating a pepperoni pizza,

I love you Mum,

Sarah xx

The significance of what I'd just seen in my vision along with the confirmation of it in Sarah's letter overwhelmed me. This was the most powerful evidence of life after death I could have given to Cathy.

And to have experienced this special moment with a mother who had lost her daughter moved me beyond words. As I stood up from the sofa, Cathy gave me a hug and thanked me. "You're a very special young man," she said.

When you are involved in an experience like this, it changes you. But, when you have experiences like these every day, it gives you a completely different perspective on life.

You no longer merely believe in the afterlife, you *know* it exists.

CHAPTER 10

Grandad Joe

One night I decided to go to the Spiritualist church. Feeling the economic pinch, I had the grand total of five pounds in my pocket until my next payday. I had to make it last. Fortunately for me, it was only a pound to attend the church's Thursday night evening of clairvoyance. And I felt unusually drawn to be there that evening.

I walked the thirty minutes from my home to the church and as I got to the door, they said, "That'll be five pounds please."

"What? It's only a pound, isn't it?"

"Not tonight. It's a special. We have three mediums on tonight and they'll be on until 9:00 pm."

I had definitely felt drawn to go that evening, but five pounds was all I had.

I needed to make a decision and fast, the church was filling up and there was a queue of people waiting behind me.

I decided on a quick excuse. "Erm, I'm just waiting for someone, I'll be back in a moment."

Now, I intended to leave and head back home. I managed to get one foot outside the church door and onto the step outside, when whoosh!

A huge rush of energy filled my stomach.

I couldn't move, I was frozen to the spot. It felt like hundreds of butterflies in my stomach. I couldn't leave for the life of me. I had an overwhelming feeling telling me to go back inside and take a seat.

Feeling a little embarrassed I went back inside and said, "Just one please," hoping they wouldn't ask about the non-existent person I was waiting for.

Once inside, I spotted an empty seat on the front row. I darted towards it and took my place.

It was 7:30 pm and the service started. The chairperson stood and welcomed everyone, then introduced each medium, thanking the third medium, Gary, for stepping in at the last minute and having come straight from work to be there.

There was a real sense of anticipation in the room. Somehow I just knew something special was happening.

The first two mediums stood in turn and gave their messages to people in the congregation. It was nice to watch and listen to people receiving messages from the platform but I had seen this happen many times before.

Why had I felt so compelled to be here?

Gary, the medium who had stepped in at the last minute, caught my attention.

I'd never seen this medium before and as the other two worked I noticed he sat with a pen and note pad in his hands, writing things down and seemingly chatting to spirit people that no one else could see. There was a strong sense of the spirit world around this man as he sat and talked to them.

I was fascinated by this.

Then he stood up. "This message is for someone who bought a new soap pump today. The gentleman in the spirit world who is coming forward is your father."

A hand went up in the room. "I can take that Gary."

"No you can't. Sorry, I'm not with you. I'm over here."

Wow!

I'd never seen a medium do that before. He then looked to the other side of the church and delivered his message to the correct recipient.

He was confident.

Assured.

And his messages were spot on.

At this stage of my development, I hadn't realized that there was such a thing as "message grabbers." Those are people who will attend an evening of clairvoyance and put up their hand every time the medium speaks in an attempt to grab a message from the other side, even if the message is not for them. I still find it extraordinary that some people think they'll actually get a message from someone else's relatives by doing this!

Each time Gary delivered a message to someone, the presence of the spirit world grew stronger in the room, it was quite an amazing feeling.

There was no beating about the bush with this guy, he gave exact names and dates, the lot.

Gary demonstrated total conviction in his messages and who they belonged to.

The other mediums seemed to pale in comparison to Gary. That's not to say they weren't good mediums, they were simply working to the limits of their ability.

He sat down and the other mediums continued to pass on messages.

"I wonder if he'll come to me." I thought.

Gary sat with his pen and note pad and once again began making notes as he chatted to spirit people. Again, I watched as he did this. Suddenly he glanced up and looked straight at me, then carried on making notes.

The other mediums completed their messages and took their seats. As Gary stood, that feeling I'd experienced on the door step outside the church returned.

"Young man I'm coming to you! I have a gentleman here, he's telling me he's your great-grandfather. He suffered with a stroke, he died when he was in his seventies. Oh, and he loved only Cadbury's dairy milk chocolate."

I knew without a doubt it was my great-grandfather, Joseph. Grandad Joe to me.

I'd had a number of relatives come through in other messages previously, but my great-grandfather had never come through before.

"I'm being shown here that you work in an office surrounded by computers."

"That's right I do."

I hadn't dressed up to come to the service. I was just wearing jeans and a t-shirt, I certainly didn't look like I worked in an office.

"The environment is very stressful. It's not right for you. You need to find another job."

He was right about that, too.

"Although your finances are a bit tight at the moment and you have to tighten your belt, things will get much better. Spirit are looking after you."

Phew, I thought. That's good news after donating the last five pounds I had at the door.

"Your great-grandfather says that you need to get yourself a new pair of shoes."

That got everyone in the church laughing, including me. I did need new shoes, mine had holes in the bottom of them!

What a fabulous demonstration of mediumship. I was so glad I had listened to the inner voice that had prompted me to be there that evening.

When the mediums left the platform, I shook hands with Gary and thanked him for my message.

Gary had a further message for me, "I know you are aware of Spirit. You've got the potential to develop that and become a great medium. You just need to practice."

Those words really stayed with me, and practice I did, at every single given opportunity.

CHAPTER 11

Ye Olde Man & Scythe

England is full of historic old buildings. It's one of the reasons we get so many people visiting the UK. There is something to be said for the centuries of history, of the people who lived here during those hundreds, even thousands of years.

As I continued developing as a medium, I also spent a great deal of time studying the subject of the supernatural. If there were a book to be found on a particular area of supernatural phenomena, you could guarantee I already had it on my bookshelf.

Mediums are often called in to deal with various different kinds of unexplained phenomena, and I always felt it was important to educate myself as much as possible on the subject. For me, investigating these occurrences was a natural extension of my ability to connect with the spirit world.

Unfortunately, the majority of television shows that cover this subject have given people the completely wrong idea of what it means to communicate with Spirit. There is a distinct difference between ghost phenomena and what a medium experiences during spirit communication.

Now to be clear, spirits are not ghosts.

Ghosts are not spirits.

Spirit people are alive. They are the living consciousness that survives after the human body dies. They retain the personality, memories, and experiences that they had while alive on the earth. Spirit people are conscious of what has been and what is happening now.

Ghosts however, are more like a filmstrip, an imprint left in space and time. They're merely a memory, a recording in the atmosphere.

They are not living, nor are they conscious.

You cannot communicate with a ghost any more than you can with an actor on a movie screen. It is not fully understood what triggers ghost phenomena to occur, but when it does, we can observe the replaying of an event that took place at some point in the past. This seems to happen whenever a living person appears on the site of that memory, acting almost like a battery that starts the projector rolling.

One of the most well documented ghost sightings in the UK was witnessed in February 1953 by Harry Martindale. It took place in the cellar beneath the Treasurer's House in the ancient city of York.

Martindale worked as an apprentice plumber and was in the process of making alterations to a central heating unit in the cellar beneath the house.

Whilst working on a ladder, he heard the distinctive sound of a musical note, the sound gradually got louder and louder. He quickly realized that the sound actually came from out of the cellar wall, which was some six feet thick.

As he glanced down from the ladder he was working on, he saw a figure wearing a helmet emerge from the stone wall. Shocked, Martindale stepped back off the ladder, fell to the ground, and scarpered to the corner of the room.

To his surprise, he looked directly at an almost fully formed Roman soldier. The soldier walked away from the wall immediately followed by a large horse that had another Roman soldier mounted on its back.

As if this sight were not paralyzing enough, several more pairs of soldiers followed, all emerging side by side from the cellar wall. They all marched in line together.

Martindale saw them in the minutest detail. He could see their armor, their swords, and even the look of exhaustion and stubble on their unshaven faces.

However, there was one very bizarre feature that really stood out. All of them could only be seen from the knees up. The lower part of their legs seemed to be missing, or embedded into the cellar floor as they marched through.

There was one small part of the cellar floor that had been excavated, right down to an old Roman road that ran directly beneath it. Interestingly enough it was only when the ghostly soldiers reached this part of the cellar that they could be seen in their entirety, from the feet upwards. They appeared to be walking on the original Roman road, which was around eighteen inches beneath the current level of the cellar floor.

The soldiers appeared so solid and lifelike that Martindale was petrified in case they turned and saw him sitting there. But, he needn't have worried. What he was observing was ghost phenomena, a recording in time.

෴

In my pursuit of supernatural experiences, I visited many old buildings that had a history. Specifically, I wanted to conduct a paranormal investigation in one of the oldest buildings in Bolton, Ye Olde Man & Scythe located at 6-8 Churchgate Bolton, Lancashire BL1 1HL. If you are not familiar with it, look it up. Established in 1251, it is over eight hundred years old, and has maintained much of the old world charm that I find so appealing.

When I landed on Ye Olde Man & Scythe, I could feel that there was something special about the place.

Rumor had it there had been a lot of unexplained activity at this location, shadows on the CCTV cameras, spirit lights, and other unexplained phenomena. I approached the landlady and asked if she would allow me to conduct an investigation in the building.

At first, she was a little unsure about me investigating her beloved public house. She then explained that one night she had come into the pub and had seen her dad standing at the end of the bar, this was some time *after* he died.

I assured her that the investigation would be done with the upmost respect for both the spirit world and the historical building. I explained that not only was I an investigator of unexplained phenomena, I was also a medium from the local Spiritualist church.

I suspect that this gave me a little bit of standing, because she gave me permission to run the investigation inside the building, half of which was a public house and the other half a spiritual shop that sold a whole host of unique and unusual things, aptly named Ye Olde Wench & Trinkets. There were also a couple of little rooms upstairs above the shop.

The investigation went very well and after completing it, the landlady asked me if I would be interested in renting one of the rooms above the shop to do my readings one day a week. I didn't have to think too long, the entire building had a good feeling to it and the room upstairs at the front had a largish window that let in a good amount of light.

I loved the crooked narrow stairs that led up to the room, and once on the landing at the top you could peer into the room through its tiny doorway. People were certainly a lot smaller eight hundred years ago, I had to duck to enter the room.

Once inside, I found the room to be crooked and tilted to one side. It was likely the most unusual room I'd seen in this very old building. Much of the original wood darkened with age was showing between the white plastered walls. I could feel the presence of Spirit with me and it seemed like the perfect place for me to conduct my readings.

I sent out a thought to the other side, just to see if they had anything to say regarding my decision to use this place as my office for private readings. I don't make a habit of consulting the spirit world over everyday decisions that I make in life, but if it's something that is going to directly involve Spirit, I always make a point of asking them what their thoughts are.

If ever they give me the feeling to walk away from a situation, I always listen. There have been times in the past when I have ignored that inner voice, with disastrous results.

But in this case, I received a message of strong approval.

The shop downstairs was run by Becky, the shop manager and all-around help. She did pretty much everything there. To get me started, she put a folding sign out on the pavement in front of the store letting people know that a medium was inside on Saturdays giving readings.

The very first Saturday I was there, I rather expected to just sit there, looking out the window, watching the world go by. But I hadn't been there for more than a couple of minutes when I learned that I had a woman there for a reading. She had just walked in and was ready.

After my first reading in my new office, I went out to get a bite of lunch. Ye Olde Pastie Shoppe, Est. 1667 was right across the street, and it soon became my regular haunt, so to speak.

When I returned, I had a second reading scheduled.

Within a couple of weeks, every Saturday was completely booked, and when the bookings extended out for three or four weeks at a time, I had to add more days.

⚜

After the success of my initial paranormal investigation, it was suggested that they be opened up to the general public and held on a monthly basis.

It wasn't long before they took on a life of their own.

Simply by word of mouth, my monthly all night investigations within Ye Olde Man & Scythe and Ye Old Wench & Trinkets were completely booked. They were one of the most popular activities in town. We used tape recorders, digital cameras, and observed live footage from the night vision CCTV. I brought a whole host of original Spiritualist paraphernalia from the past to conduct experiments and hold séance communications with the spirit world.

If I had read about it, I would experiment with it. I soon discovered what worked well and what didn't.

We would meet late, around 10:30 in the evening, starting the first part of the investigation in the shop as the other side of the building was a working public house and their hours extended to midnight. After midnight, we would leave Ye Olde Wench & Trinkets and enter Ye Old Man & Scythe.

At the start of each investigation, we headed upstairs to my office. As we stood in a circle, I asked people what feelings they had, what they sensed. Everyone was encouraged to take photos or videos, whatever they wanted. Many spirit lights would show up in the photos.

During the investigation, I always made a point of explaining to everyone that the spirit people who were most likely to make an appearance were their own family members. I encouraged them to speak to them just as they always would, when they are addressed this way, their interaction is far more likely.

We are always surrounded by the spirits of our family and friends, and they enjoy having that connection with us as we go about our daily activities.

Back downstairs was a fairy room. Not real fairies, mind you. It was just a room full of fairies, everywhere. Some in glass jars. Some extended from the ceiling. There were hundreds of them hanging from strings. Many people experienced feelings in that room, ghostly memories still present from long ago. It was also quite common to hear footsteps and bangs coming from upstairs whilst standing in the fairy room.

In the case of a building like Ye Olde Man & Scythe, there is great potential for a whole range of supernatural occurrences to take place. One, because of the sheer number of years that it has stood on that location for, and because of the tense and dramatic history that is has. James Stanley the 7th Earl of Derby spent his last moments in Ye Olde Man & Scythe immediately prior to his execution on October 15th 1651.

The more emotionally charged a memory is, the more likely its ghost will replay.

As a public house, frequented daily by living members of the public, this particular building has the potential for a lot of spirit connection too, and not just the ones behind the bar!

For our supernatural investigations, Ye Olde Man & Scythe provided the perfect location. Everyone enjoyed the sessions, which usually lasted for over six or seven hours.

Imagine my amazement when the most negative feedback I got had to do with how *short* the sessions were!

SHORT?

We spent the whole night investigating that very special location.

Those were very fun times.

CHAPTER 12

Sixth Sense or Nonsense?

I n all walks of life you will come across nonsense at some point. But the world of mediums, spirits, and the paranormal seems to attract more than its fair share.

One day I arrived at a house to conduct a private reading. A pleasant lady with a warm smile answered the door. When I stepped inside I immediately noticed how cold the house was. As I followed her into the living room an icy cold chill swept past us both. When we entered the kitchen it grew even colder still.

My client turned to me and said, "I hope I've done everything right for you. I've had the electricity switched off for twenty-four hours and opened every window in the house to let the spirits in."

"I'm sorry, I'm not sure I understand."

Inside, I was thinking, that's bizarre, and why on earth have you done that???

She was a sincere and intelligent woman. Unfortunately, her only experience with having a reading was with a card reader who required these bizarre and completely nonsensical rituals.

Knowledge is power, but "nonsense knowledge" can affect even the most credible of people.

This woman in all earnestness believed that she needed to perfect my environment with these strange rituals before I could make contact with her loved ones in the spirit world.

I learned early on, that many of the so-called "traditions," "rituals," and "necessary preparations" are nothing more than old wives' tales and superstition.

I'd like to dedicate this chapter to dispelling the myths, misconceptions, and sheer nonsense that all too often surrounds the subject of mediumship, spirits, and the afterlife.

Go Into the Light?

When we pass over and make our transition to the spirit world, there is always someone who comes to greet you, regardless of how you pass, what beliefs you may have, or how you've lived your life.

This can be a loved one or close friend, but is usually someone who is special to you, who you will instantly recognize. This is evident from the countless messages that come through from spirit people during readings and public demonstrations of mediumship.

There is no such thing as a person being trapped between worlds or being unable to "go into the light."

You are either in this world or the next.

There is no in-between or getting lost along the way.

I have heard of rescue circles that specialize in helping trapped or lost souls to cross over. I'm sure they are sincere groups of likeminded people with only good intentions.

But, my question is this, if every person who passes is greeted by a loved one on the other side, then how can it be possible to get lost or not be able to get into the spirit world? There is not a medium alive who knows more about the other side than the spirits who are already there. If any help was needed to cross over, it would come from the spirit world, *not* from us.

Protection

In the world of mediums, you are sure to come across the subject of protection.

Spiritual protection, to be exact.

Strangely enough, there are many people out there who believe that the spirit world is so dangerous that you must protect yourself before you attempt to communicate with it.

But protect yourself with what?

And from what?

Spirit are with us every minute of the day, whether or not the medium is working, whether or not we are aware of their presence. It really makes no sense to protect yourself just when you want to talk to them and not at any other time.

You needn't worry, you don't need to protect yourself from the presence of Spirit.

Opening Up

In order for a medium to communicate with the spirit world, there is only one thing they need to do. This involves calming the mind and allowing it to be relaxed and receptive so that it can receive impressions from the spirit world.

In this receptive daydream state, the communication process is much easier as it isn't interrupted by the mediums own thoughts that can get in the way.

This mental process of calming the mind should be simple and, to a developed medium, second nature.

In my early stages of development, I came across many teachers and circle leaders who added so many rituals, routines, and nonsense to this very simple process that it became very confusing to me. At first, I followed these long-winded opening up rituals.

I would sit down, close my eyes and open each Chakra in the right order and with the correct colour (I know of blind mediums out there who can't see colour at all.)

Then ask my gatekeeper to open the gate.

Then my guardian angel had to be addressed before finally inviting in the spirit guide, which meant I was finally "open" and ready to work as a medium.

Confused?

So was I.

This mental process was so long and complicated I was often left feeling more jumbled up and confused rather than relaxed and receptive to Spirit.

One day whilst attending a Spiritualist church, I sat waiting for the service to start. After discovering that the medium hadn't arrived, I was asked if I wouldn't mind stepping in to take the service. Without hesitation I said, "Yes," and before I could change my mind, I was on the platform and delivering spirit messages. I'd had an enjoyable service and before I knew it, it was over. It was only afterwards whilst reflecting on the service I'd just given that I realized I hadn't gone through my opening up ritual.

Yet I had connected with the spirit world and delivered their messages without any problems. I hadn't used any of these so-called "mandatory" protocols and it would appear that I hadn't needed them.

And, I've never used them since.

All a medium needs is a calm mind and a willingness to work. If having some sort of opening up ritual puts a particular medium in the right frame of mind, it may well work for them, but it really isn't necessary.

A natural medium is aware of the spirit world and can be ready to communicate with them in a matter of seconds. It's a very simple shift in the medium's awareness that puts their mind in attunement with the spirit world.

Uncross Your Arms and Legs

Have you ever heard a medium say you must uncross your legs and unfold your arms before they can give you a message? If not, you're in luck, but if you have then you may well be wondering why they said that and you wouldn't be the only one.

The spirit world is non-physical.

You cannot stop or block a spirit message from coming through based on the way you happen to be sitting. Many times, I have given messages to people with physical disabilities in which it would be impossible for them to either fold or unfold their arms and legs. Their disability had no impact on the spirit person's connection or the messages that came through in any way.

It doesn't matter how you sit. If Spirit have a message for you they will pass it on regardless of your posture!

Voice Vibration

On the subject of blocking or stopping spirit people from coming through, it is often said that the medium must hear the recipient's voice because spirit work on a *"voice vibration."*

This is also untrue.

I have given spirit messages to people who were completely deaf or were unable to speak at all. As I delivered their message, a signer would interpret using sign language, passing on the information to the recipient who would then acknowledge and confirm the message that I was giving.

The lack of the recipient's voice had no impact on the communication process with Spirit. The connection was just as strong as any other reading that I've experienced.

Pregnant Women Can't Have Readings

Erm, yes they can.

I have read for many pregnant ladies.

On some occasions, spirit people even give information regarding the new arrival, their sex, their name, and even their due date.

Spirit people love babies just as much as we do and they are often present at the birth of a new child.

Hungry Medium

Mediums must fast before working with the spirit world.

Really?

Well actually, no.

They can if they so wish, but I don't see how this can enhance the mediumship in any way. It's an old-fashioned ritual that many of the old mediums used to adhere to, and some mediums still use today. In my early days, I followed this ritual and after not eating all day, I would stand on platform to deliver messages, but found that the only thing it helped my mind to focus on was my grumbling empty stomach.

In my early twenties, many of my church demonstrations would end with me in the tea room overindulging on biscuits to fill my ravenous stomach.

"You're Holding Them Back"

I once held a reading for a lady who had very tragically lost her son. It was one of the most emotional and healing connections from the other side.

Towards the end of the reading, the young man in spirit said that his mother had been told not to think about him anymore, and that she must let him go. He also mentioned just how much this had upset his mother.

"Has someone told you that you must stop thinking about your son?" I asked the mother.

"Yes, I have been trying my best not to think about Michael, but I just can't help it. He's my son."

I asked who had given such advice to this grieving mother.

"One of the nurses in the hospital told me that if I hold onto his memory and keep thinking about him, it will stop him from progressing in the spirit world."

What a load of nonsense!

As if losing a child isn't hard enough, can you imagine what it must be like to be told that you shouldn't think about them or hold onto them in any way after they have gone? This is a widely held belief by many people regarding the subject of the afterlife.

We are given the ability to love for a reason. To suggest that you can turn this love "off" once that person has died is ridiculous.

It's very natural to want that connection with someone you have loved and lost. It's all part of the grieving process and is a necessary part of our own progress in this world.

You cannot stop a loved one on the other side from progressing on their spiritual journey in any way. Your loved ones want you to know that they are still nearby and will always be a part of your life.

Love them, miss them, and talk to them every day if you need to. Nothing will hold them back.

Demons and Devils

Are mediums talking to demons, pretending to be our relatives on the other side?

I get this one quite often, so many people must believe it.

The short answer is, no.

There are no such things as demons. And if there were, why on earth would a demon want to bring comfort and joy to someone by pretending to be their granny? They are supposed to do bad things aren't they?

And the Devil?

A big red guy with horns tempting people to do bad things? I don't think so.

People must take personal responsibility for their own lives, the decisions they make, and the actions they carry out. To blame bad things on a mythical horned being who lives under the ground in a world of fire is almost as bad as, in fact worse than saying, "It wasn't me, he made me do it."

The truth is, when people do bad things they are responsible for what they do, not devils.

Do Spirits Watch Me in the Shower?

This is a question I get time and time again from some very worried members of the public. If spirit people are watching over us as we go about our daily lives, you may wonder just how much of our daily lives they get to see? Quite often during readings, spirit people will mention what they have seen us doing. For example, writing birthday cards, having new furniture fitted, or even what we ate for breakfast.

They mention these things to show us that they really are still a part of our lives and that they haven't left us.

But, do they watch me in the shower?

The answer is, "NO!"

When we cross over, we leave our physical bodies behind. All thoughts and feelings that are connected to having a physical body are also left behind. The body is meaningless to a spirit person.

There are no peeping Toms in the spirit world.

I have on some occasions had spirit people come and chat to me whilst in the shower or whilst I've been relaxing and meditating in the bathtub. But this is because I am most relaxed and receptive at those times, not because they want to peek at me. They have no interest in spying on us or our bodies!

What Happens if You Separate the Ashes of a Loved One?

Nothing at all.

The spirit is separate from the body. After the transition to the spirit world has taken place, spirit people have no connection to the body whatsoever. They don't care what happens to it.

A spirit lady once said that she felt the same way about her body as she did about her hair on the floor after a visit to the hairdressers.

Once her hair was done, all she was interested in was what she could see in the mirror, not what was being swept up on the salon floor. She no longer associated the hair on the floor as being a part of her, and it was the same with her body.

Final Thoughts

Throughout my development as a medium, I have personally encountered all of the myths, rituals, and nonsense that I have addressed in this chapter. I can say with the upmost honesty that none of them, in my experience, are either necessary or true.

When it comes to the subject of mediumship and the afterlife, my advice is to keep an open mind, keep it simple, and use common sense. Always be prepared to question and re-evaluate your beliefs, whatever they may be.

CHAPTER 13

Spirit of Laughter

One of our most defining characteristics that identifies us as human is our ability to laugh. The human spirit has always found ways to deal with the most difficult of situations and laughter is one of our most prized mechanisms for doing this.

I've always found laughter to be an amazing and powerful source of healing, in more ways than one.

It's an energy that has the power to change the atmosphere even in the gloomiest of situations.

And sometimes we don't know why something is funny.

It just is.

I'd like to dedicate this chapter to some of the more fun and at times outright hilarious situations I've ended up in whilst working with Spirit.

The Frightened Spiritualists

Once I was giving a demonstration of mediumship at a Spiritualist church in Leigh. It was the last place you would expect a group of people to become frightened of the spirit world.

I was in the process of delivering a spirit message to a woman in the congregation when half way through her message I said, "You don't believe a word I'm saying do you?"

"Erm, not really, I'm quite sceptical about these things," she replied.

Immediately I became aware of the spirit world rushing forward to give their own response to the situation. It happened so quickly that before I could interpret the feelings I was receiving I only got the chance to say, "Watch the lights."

Immediately the church plunged into darkness as the lights went out. I heard loud gasps and some screams from the congregation before the lights came back on.

"There are over a hundred Spiritualists in here tonight and that's how you react when a spirit turns out the lights?" I remarked from the platform. Everybody looked at each other before roaring with laughter.

If you've ever wondered why spirits don't materialize physically during a public demonstration of mediumship, I think you'll find that this is the answer. It was the last place I expected to hear shouts and screams when a spirit made its presence known.

Billy One-Leg

Occasionally spirit people come through from the other side with a message that's so uplifting it not only cheers up the person receiving the message, but everyone in the room becomes involved.

It was during a theatre demonstration of mediumship when I became aware of two spirit people, one a lady, the other a gentleman and both of them were communicating at the same time. I heard the gentleman introduce himself as "Billy."

As the spirit lady began to communicate I became aware of the fact that she had lost one of her legs before she had passed away. More details came through, and a woman in the audience raised her hand and accepted the message.

It was her mother in spirit coming through. The woman confirmed that her mother had indeed lost a leg, but she didn't know who "Billy" was.

"That's okay," I said as I continued to connect with her mother. The sensation of a missing leg became so strong I said with absolute confidence, "Your mum lost her left leg didn't she?"

"No, it was the other one" the woman replied.

I was a little stunned as I could feel the sensation of my left leg missing to the point where I was certain.

Just then, the gentleman who had connected with me at the start of the message began to draw very close. As he did I could feel that he also had a leg missing.

His left one to be exact.

"I have a gentleman coming through, and believe it or not he has a leg missing as well, it's his left one."

His presence was the reason I'd got the missing leg mixed up just a few moments ago.

"No, I don't know of anyone like that," the woman replied.

It was the first time I'd ever had two spirit people come through together, one with their right leg missing the other with their left.

The thought of them being a matching pair crossed my mind, but before I had the chance to vocalize that thought the woman receiving the message shouted, "OH . . . BILLY ONE-LEG!"

The whole theatre erupted with laughter.

"Remember at the start of the message when I said I had a man coming through introducing himself as Billy?"

"I didn't know he'd died!" Another wave of laughter swept through the audience.

"Well, I hate to be the one to break the news to you, sweetheart but . . ."

The theatre again erupted with laughter. Finally the laughter subsided and the woman's mother came back to pass on just one last message.

"Your mother is still here and she wants to leave you with her love and . . . she's . . . taking out her dentures and placing them in a little plastic tub?" After the two missing legs, I wondered what on earth this last part of the message meant.

To my surprise the woman said, "Yes, my mum wore dentures and I've brought her denture tub with me tonight!"

The woman reached into her handbag and produced the denture tub, held it up in the air, and rattled it for the whole theatre to see.

"What have you brought that for?" I asked in disbelief.

At this point, the laughter took on a life of its own as it enveloped the audience. Even I began to lose my composure. I sat back in my chair on the stage and along with the audience cried with laughter until my sides hurt.

It was obvious to me that her mother in the spirit world had found the connection with Billy One-Leg just as funny as we all had and so decided to join in and bring some laughter of her own. A wonderful feeling filled the theatre after that connection. Spirit people are anything but gloomy or depressed.

The fun and laughter they bring through with them is a reflection of the life they lead on the other side.

The Honest Lady

I'd just delivered a spirit message to one lovely lady in a theatre audience. Her father had come through and given his exact name followed by her mother who also gave her exact name. As more information came through, the lady in the audience spoke clearly into the microphone she was holding and confirmed her message.

When her message was complete, I gave her a rose and thanked her for working so openly with me. As I reached for a glass of water on the stage, this lovely lady leaned over to her partner sitting at the side of her, apparently forgetting that she still had a live microphone in her hand, and whispered, "You know when I said I thought he was shite, well, he's actually really good."

Well, I guess there's nothing like saying it as it is. But, this little whisper came through the microphone quite clearly and with plenty of volume, resulting in thunderous laughter and applause from the audience.

Wii-Fit Sceptic

Whilst holding a joint private reading for a husband and wife in their home I came up against one of the most irritatingly sceptical people I'd ever read for.

Each time I brought through some evidence from the other side the woman would say, "Wow that's my mum's name, or that's amazing, she did live in Wales."

However, for all the evidence the spirit world were able to get through, each time I spoke the gentleman rolled his eyes, huffed his breath, and folded his arms in what seemed like an effort to thwart everything I said.

After about fifteen constant minutes of this, I finally asked him what he was so miffed about.

He grunted and said that he was less than impressed by what he was hearing and that I needed to give him something more concrete if he was to be convinced. "If my mother-in-law is really talking to you, can she tell you what I was doing in this house before you arrived?"

The moment he asked this question I was shown a vision I'll never forget. (It's one of those things you simply cannot *un*-see!)

"You were on the Wii-Fit machine doing a workout," I said.

"That's obvious," he groaned, as he folded his arms. "You can plainly see that we've got a Wii-Fit. It's right there in front of the telly."

"Yes," I paused, then said, "but you were naked weren't you?"

The man instantly fell silent. His face changed from a pale white to a fierce shade of crimson. Abruptly he stood and then walked out of the room in total silence.

As he walked out his wife shouted after him, "I told you my mother would be watching!"

I Know My Brother

Sometimes, when a medium is working, they get things wrong. Misinterpreting a birthday for an anniversary, or a daffodil for a dandelion . . . But some things that are said during a reading are either blatantly right or blatantly wrong. I was just coming to the end of an exceptionally clear and detailed private reading. The brother of the woman for whom I was reading had come through from the other side with such strength he managed to get his first and middle name across, his birthday, and even the street he'd grown up on.

As the reading was drawing to a close I saw a picture of him in my mind.

"He's showing me a picture of himself, he has ginger hair."

"Yes, that's right."

"He's wearing a police officer's uniform."

"Yes, he was in the police."

I was on a roll of spiritual energy as I continued, "And he's got a moustache."

"No. He never had a moustache!" She stopped me in my tracks.

"Are you sure?" I asked.

"Of course I'm sure, I knew my brother for thirty-eight years, and he never once had a moustache."

Her conviction was strong.

Who was I to question it?

After completing the reading, she gave me a hug and thanked me for her message even though I'd mistakenly given her brother a moustache.

"I've got a picture of him in my purse. Would you like to see it?" She asked.

"Sure," I said.

She reached into her purse and handed the photo over. It was an ID card belonging to her brother, with a picture of him wearing his police uniform attached to it. The moment I saw it, I couldn't help but notice something obvious.

A great big ginger moustache!

"Have you seen that sitting on your brother's top lip?" I pointed at the picture.

She looked and gasped, "OH, YEAH! Well, I never noticed that." Her brother in spirit must have been wondering why on earth she said no to his most distinguishing feature.

The Toilet Brush

When demonstrating mediumship in front of a large audience I always ask the spirit people to be as specific as possible with the details they come through with. This way it eliminates many hands going up and I spend less time locating the correct recipient of the message.

On one such occasion, the spirit person coming through decided to give a very specific, but rather embarrassing, detail. To accept the message meant that one young man in the audience had no choice but to own up to an event that had happened just moments before leaving home to come to the theatre. "I've got a gentleman in spirit, and he's telling me that this message is for someone who has just recently blocked up their toilet, he's seen you forcing a toilet brush down it today."

I'd never started a spirit message like this before. For a few moments no one put up their hand as I scanned the room for a response.

To be perfectly honest, I didn't expect anyone to accept this message.

But to my surprise, and that of the audience, a rather red faced young man put up his hand and confessed, "I did that today."

Several members of his family seated on the same row all leaned out of their seats to look at him in disbelief. At least he was honest enough to accept such a precise message, even if he did have some explaining to do when he got home.

Tea or Coffee?

My wife had booked in a client for a private reading, which would take place at her home. During a phone call to confirm the appointment, the client mentioned that she was an extremely nervous person, especially around men.

Her statement seemed rather odd and as a precaution, I decided to take my wife along with me.

When we arrived at the house all seemed well, at least from the outside of the house.

"Everything seems okay. I can feel Spirit, so there must be a reason for me being here. I think I'll be fine, you wait here in the car, any problems and I'll come and get you," I said to my wife.

I knocked on the door and after a short while, it opened just a nick. Two eyes looked out at me from the small gap behind the door.

"Hi, it's David. You have a reading booked at 10:00 am. Have you forgotten?"

"No, I've just been rushing around trying to get everything to-gether, come in."

The young woman pulled back the door and shuffled back with it. I stepped inside the hallway and the door slammed shut behind me.

Standing there in the hallway was my nervous client wearing nothing more than her vest top and underwear!

"Haven't you forgotten something?" I said.

"What?"

"YOUR CLOTHES!" was my startled reply.

"Oh, sorry. I've just been rushing round all morning. Would you like a drink?"

At this point, I would normally have left if it weren't for the strong presence of a spirit lady who appeared to be the young woman's mother. Still doubtful as to whether or not this was a good idea, I cautiously took a seat in the living room.

"Tea or coffee?" She asked, while pulling on a jumper then dashing out of the room.

Hopping back into the living room on one leg with the other stuck in her jeans, "Milk and sugar?"

While making my drink the young woman bobbed in and out of the living room, each time asking a question regarding my beverage and each time pulling on another item of clothing.

To my infinite relief, she finally walked in fully clothed with my cup of tea as if nothing unusual had happened at all. She took her seat and eagerly waited for the reading to commence.

For someone who supposedly suffered from a nervous disposition, especially around men, she certainly didn't show it.

The only person who seemed nervous in that house was me!

CHAPTER 14

Magic Rope & Five Pound Note

The spirit world is all around us at all times. It isn't up in the clouds or off in some distant part of the universe. Our two worlds are opposite sides of the same coin. And with such closeness, the unseen world often finds remarkable ways of letting us know that they are there, that they can and do have an effect and influence on this world.

One such phenomenon that some have experienced is *synchronicity*. These are separate events or situations in our lives that end up coming together with such precise timing that they couldn't have happened by chance alone.

Some of these experiences send a chill down our spines and can even change the way we view our lives.

I'm sure you have already had the experience of someone popping into your thoughts, someone you haven't seen or heard from in a long while. Then immediately the phone rings and when you answer it's the very same person you were just thinking about.

Or perhaps you've been singing a song in your mind only to find that it's the next song to play on the radio?

Such instances are often brushed off as mere coincidence, but some of these events go way beyond coincidence. This is where we step into the realm of synchronicity. My first experience with this fascinating phenomenon was back in my childhood.

I was around six years old when I saw magic for the very first time. My stepfather worked as a bus driver and one of the other drivers, Billy, put on a magic show for all the children of the bus drivers.

I sat cross-legged on the floor among all the other children, waiting for Billy the Magician to start.

There were coloured silk hankies and all kinds of boxes and props. I sat patiently wondering what was going to happen with all that stuff, then Billy the Magician began his show.

I sat mesmerized.

I couldn't believe what I was seeing.

Coins vanishing, rabbits coming out of hats, and a lady being sawn in half with a chain saw! I'd never seen anything like it before. Toward the end of the show, Billy performed all kinds of amazing tricks with a rope. He would cut it and it would restore. The rope would change size, knots would appear and then vanish, and do countless other wonders.

At the end of the show Billy said, "Who wants a piece of magic rope?" My hand shot up, my arm was almost popping out of its socket as I struggled to stretch my hand as far as possible into the air. You bet I wanted a piece of that rope.

"I'm going to give you all a piece of magic rope." Billy produced a big pair of gleaming scissors and began to cut the rope into smaller pieces. One by one, he invited us up to the front to receive our piece of magic rope and then we were asked to sit quietly.

You could have heard a pin drop.

"When you go home tonight, put your magic rope underneath your pillow before you go to sleep. When you wake up in the morning it will have grown into a full length rope. If it doesn't grow, don't worry. That means you'll find a fiver instead!"

WOW!

I could hardly wait to get home and go to bed.

In my innocence, I didn't realize that this was actually a joke on the parents sitting at the back of the room. Knowing full well the rope wouldn't grow, the parents would have to place a five pound note there. And now I understand why they were all laughing when he said it.

My family was exceptionally poor, so there was no chance that was going to happen for me. I often wondered why the tooth fairy only ever left me twenty pence for my teeth when all of my friends received a pound for theirs.

Upon arriving home, I ran upstairs. Before placing the rope under my pillow, I measured it along my set of drawers and made a mark with a piece of chalk.

The following morning I woke and the excitement of what might be under the pillow was almost too much to bear. My mother stood in my doorway and watched as I lifted the pillow, grabbed the rope, and rushed over to my drawers to measure it.

"Has it grown?" Mum asked.

"No."

"Oh well, never mind, at least you got a piece to keep. Come on, I'm going to start breakfast in a minute."

My mother sounded a little disappointed for me which I didn't understand, I wasn't sad at all. The rope hadn't grown an inch which meant I was going to find a fiver! Just like Billy the Magician said.

After breakfast, my stepfather asked if I wanted to join him on the walk into town. It was windy out but at least the sun was shining so I said yes. He was picking up a film that was being processed at the camera shop.

When we arrived at the camera shop, my stepdad said, "You wait here, I won't be long."

As I stood waiting outside the camera shop, a gust of wind came rushing up the street bringing with it a mixture of leaves and empty wrappers swirling around my feet. In this whirlwind of crisp packets and litter, I could clearly see a five-pound note. I grabbed it and immediately started shouting for my stepdad.

He came out of the shop and before he could take his next breath, "Dad, Dad, look I've found a fiver, just like Billy the Magician said I would!"

"What! Where did you get that from?"

"It was right there on the pavement, it just came blowing up the street."

Being the God-fearing Catholic that he was, my stepdad snatched it out of my hand, opened the camera shop door, held the fiver up in the air and shouted "Has anyone dropped a five-pound note, my son's just found one out here."

What!!! Dad, what the heck are you doing? I thought. That's mine!

Thankfully, nobody claimed it and we began our walk home. When we got back home, we explained to my mother what had happened. After a brief family meeting, it was decided that I was allowed to keep my fiver.

As my stepdad was a bus driver I would often go to work with him and spend the day riding as his co-pilot. A week or so later whilst changing buses we spotted Billy the Magician. My stepdad called him over and explained that his prediction had come true.

Strangely, Billy, seemed to be more surprised than we were.

CHAPTER 15

Paramedics and Tissues

Those who cross over and make that journey to the other side often find ways to show us that they haven't really left us. They give signs to comfort, reassure, and demonstrate that they are still a part of our lives.

Sometimes the signs are subtle. A thought, a feeling, or even a dream. But sometimes spirit people are willing to move mountains to show their loved ones they are still near. Sometimes the signs are just too big to be missed.

One evening back in 2013, I gave a demonstration of mediumship to an audience. Whilst meditating in my dressing room, I became aware of the presence of two young ladies in the spirit world. They were both talking to each other about how they had died, even though they had never met in this world.

It was time for the demonstration and I started the evening with an apology for being a couple of minutes late on stage. I explained that I had been occupied by two young ladies in my dressing room and had lost track of time. The audience erupted with laughter, for a second I wondered what they had found so hilarious. Then it hit me, I hadn't mentioned the fact that the two ladies in my dressing room were spirit people not physical ones!

The evening commenced. Spirit people came forward and I passed on their messages to members of the audience. Just moments before the interval, the spirit of a young girl connected with me, loudly and clearly.

She told me that she had been killed in a hit-and-run accident at just thirteen-years-old. I could see her blonde hair and blue eyes. She also specified that she was wearing a pink velour tracksuit.

The information came through so quickly I struggled to keep up. A hand went up in the audience, a young woman by the name of Celina instantly recognized the details of the message.

As soon as I began to speak, Celina knew without a doubt that the blonde-haired blue-eyed girl in spirit was her very own sister,

Carla. She had indeed been killed in a hit-and-run accident nine years before.

Just moments before receiving the message Celina had experienced an extraordinary feeling of emotion rise up in her chest. It was so strong that it felt like she was burning up inside. She knew something unusual was happening.

Celina's decision to come to my demonstration that evening had been purely spur-of-the-moment. She had brought along her friend who had recently lost her father in the hope he might come through with a message. But it was Celina who was to receive a message that night.

More evidence came through and finally Carla advised her sister in the audience not to keep focusing on the person who was responsible for her death, but to focus on all the wonderful memories they'd shared together and the fun they'd had whilst making them.

Carla was now watching over her big sister from the spirit world.

The message was complete and we broke for the interval. Throughout the message, Celina wept openly. Sitting just behind her was Lindsay, a caring member of the audience who had tapped her on the shoulder during the message and handed her a tissue.

Celina and Lindsay had never met before. As people left their seats to get drinks and refreshments Lindsay asked, "Was everything he said really bob on?"

Celina nodded. "Yes, every word, that's the reason I'm so emotional. I know for certain that was my sister. The velour track suit is what did it for me."

Celina and Lindsay chatted for a moment. When the interval was over, Lindsay sat back and watched the remainder of the show with great interest. There really must be something to this life after death stuff after all.

Lindsay attended the evening with her friend and fellow workmate, Kim. They had both enjoyed their night out with the spirits, but little did they know just how significant their presence had been.

Several weeks later, Lindsay attended an emergency ambulance transfer in her work as a paramedic. Their patient, a middle-aged woman by the name of Michaela, had been admitted to Bolton Hospital with a suspected heart attack. Now she was being transported via ambulance to Wythenshawe Hospital for an angiogram.

Lindsay responded to Michaela's every medical need, but was unable to quell the woman's intense anxiety and fear of dying.

At one point, the patient said "Well, if I die, at least I'll be with my daughter."

This was the perfect opening for Lindsay to have a distracting conversation with the distraught patient. During the conversation the subject of life after death arose.

Lindsay recounted the experience she'd had in the theatre several weeks earlier.

"You know, I went to see a medium a few weeks ago with my friend, Kim. He gave a message to this young woman sitting just in front of us. He brought through the spirit of a thirteen-year-old girl who had been killed in a hit-and-run accident. It turned out that this girl was her sister. Being a mother myself, I was in tears listening to her message. I handed her a tissue and during the interval I had a chat to her."

"Was that medium David Holt?" Michaela asked.

"Yes . . ."

"THAT WAS MY DAUGHTER!" Michaela yelled.

"You're kidding! She was tall with long blonde hair." Lindsay gasped.

"That's my Celina, she told me that a kind lady had given her a tissue. Oh my God, I'm gonna call her right now."

In just a few short moments, Michaela had gone from fearing her own death to forgetting all about it. Right in the midst of an emergency ambulance ride, Michaela pulled out her mobile phone and punched in some numbers.

"Celina? Hiya, it's Mum. Guess who I'm with?"

"Er, I don't know Mum, I thought you were in an ambulance? Is it a celebrity?"

"No, well yes. Almost. Do you remember the woman who gave you the tissue at the show when our Carla came through?

"Yes."

"That's who I'm with. She's the paramedic who's with me in the ambulance, the very same woman!"

Of all the messages that Lindsay could have recalled from the evening, she happened to talk about the one involving Carla's spirit to her patient, who was Carla's mother!

They were all stunned by the extraordinary synchronicity they'd just experienced, but it was about to take an even stranger twist.

When Lindsay explained what had happened in the ambulance to her friend Kim, the same friend she had attended the demonstration of mediumship with, a shiver came over her.

Kim's husband, Simon, also a paramedic, had been the one who attended the scene of Carla's hit-and-run accident nine years before.

Synchronicity is one of the many ways that Spirit can show us just how close they are.

A simple act of compassion, such as handing someone a tissue, can lead to amazing and sometimes life changing experiences.

Spirit underwrite a lot of the experiences that we have in this world. Whether or not we choose to acknowledge them, is up to us.

CHAPTER 16

Kelly's Story

The role of a medium is to make contact with the spirit world, to bring through evidence of life after death, and pass on any messages that the spirit people wish to convey.

However, there are times when Spirit bring messages that pertain to the future, these messages can only be verified with the passage of time.

The following story is one of the most fascinating cases I've been involved with when it comes to seeing into the future. The precision of the details that Spirit provided regarding future events was breathtaking.

A new client, by the name of Kelly, had arranged for a private reading at a friend's house.

The presence of Spirit was particularly strong when I arrived, and the moment Kelly took her seat in front of me, the reading began.

I immediately picked up on Kelly's grandparents. In particular, it was her grandfather who initiated the communication, and he did so with the upmost precision.

I saw a man with sharp features and keen eyes, the kind of man who seemed to see right through you. Wearing a smart black uniform with shiny buttons and a hat, he really had a look of authority about him.

"That sounds just like my grandfather, he was a police inspector back in the 1950's, I have a picture of him in that uniform," Kelly said.

As Kelly described the photograph, I heard a man's voice clearly say, "Bob."

"That's definitely my grandad, his name was Bob!"

I then saw a vision of a special medal he'd worn. I described it in the best way I could. Kelly had several medals belonging to her grandfather back at home. I grabbed a sheet of paper from the table and drew what I could see. The vision was so vivid and clear I could see every detail. Kelly didn't have the medal with her, but when she got home and compared the medals to the drawing I'd done, one of them was a perfect match. During the reading, her grandfather instructed her to hold onto that medal.

As the reading continued, her grandfather told me that Kelly had suffered a very serious accident and was lucky to be walking. He said he was looking after her that day and that she was extremely lucky her head had been protected.

Kelly had only just returned to work after a year's absence, recovering. She'd been thrown from a horse and broken her back. Just as her grandfather said, her head had been protected by the riding helmet she wore.

The evidence her grandfather conveyed amazed Kelly. Everything he said was meticulously detailed; his name, uniform, medals, and even the accident.

I enjoyed the communication with Bob. Everything he said was so precise, and Kelly could immediately validate the information he gave each time something came through. I suppose it was this attention to detail that had given him such good standing in his role as police inspector.

Just as I was happy and comfortable with this communication Kelly's reading took a very different turn.

"Your life seems to have no direction at the moment, but you're not to worry, your grandad Bob is helping you. I'm being told that you're going to have a baby within two years. This child is going to be special, and the arrival of this little one is going to be very good for you, a complete new start in life."

"A baby?" Kelly gasped.

I wasn't aware that she had recently ended her relationship and was more than happy to stay single.

The next thing I picked up was that Kelly would be moving house. Her grandad showed me a For Sale sign indicating the move.

Again, she looked surprised and confused. She had just returned to work after her injury and was living with her mum. She planned to continue living there while she saved some much needed funds. The last thing on her mind was moving house.

However, considering the strong evidence that her grandfather had given at the start of the reading Kelly listened attentively to every word.

"I'm being given the name Johnathan, although it doesn't mean anything to you now, it will. I'm being told the connection with that name is important, make sure you write it down. The month of July is also important. It's going to be cause for a big celebration. In fact, the eighteenth is extremely significant."

Kelly sat there politely and listened to me come out with one big statement after another. Her expression was a mixture of amazement, disbelief, and wonder all at the same time. Although each part of the message seemed to be the complete opposite of Kelly's current situation, she dutifully wrote everything down.

It was only later on that she revealed that her initial thoughts were; "You've got to be kidding. There's no way I'm having a baby in the next two years. I've just split up with my boyfriend, and I'm happy to be single. I want to travel, and enjoy life before I settle down, get married, and eventually have children. I know for certain that this is my grandad Bob, but this part just seems way off."

Once the reading was over, I thanked Kelly and left.

Had it not been for a frantic phone call some eight weeks later, I'd probably have forgotten all about my reading with Kelly.

My wife listened to a number of answer phone messages requesting private readings when a frantic female voice caught her attention.

"Oh my God, I just had to phone you," (deep breath) . . . you did a reading for me and I wasn't gonna move house but I did move," (several short breaths) "then you said the eighteenth and the contraception hasn't worked and . . . grandad Bob said" . . . (a flurry of words and short breaths that neither of us could make out) . . . "and I'M HAVING A BABY..!!!"

After listening to the message several times, we finally got the gist of what the woman was trying to say. Curious about what had happened, I called her back.

When she calmed down, I realized that it was the same Kelly that I'd read for a couple of months ago. But what she had to say was astonishing.

In just eight weeks, Kelly's life had changed dramatically.

Shortly after having the reading, she tried to help one of her friends find a tenant for a house she wanted to rent out.

Kelly knew someone who seemed like the perfect tenant.

However, after hooking them up, the deal fell through and the house remained empty. After seeing pictures of the house online, Kelly decided she rather liked the look of the property herself and arranged to view it.

The moment she stepped inside, she fell in love with the place. The location was perfect, without a second thought, Kelly acted on impulse and moved in.

Shortly after moving in to her new home, Kelly met Johnathon. Their relationship was brief, and despite taking every step to prevent a pregnancy, Kelly discovered that she was expecting her first child. Now alone and pregnant for the first time, Kelly was upset, anxious, and confided in one of her friends.

"Didn't that medium say something about a baby when you had a reading a few months back?" asked her friend.

In the midst of all her stress, Kelly couldn't recall the details of the reading but remembered that she had written notes. She searched until she found her notebook and read her notes. As she turned the pages, she could hardly believe what she was reading.

"Will have a baby within two years – special."

Kelly sat in shock with her jaw open as she read through each line.

"Moving house."

Kelly's heart started to beat faster the more she read. Then, she read something that she had completely forgotten about, a name. A name that she had been instructed to write down.

"Johnathan."

This name hadn't meant anything to her at the time of the reading. But, the name I had told her to write down was the name of the father to her unborn child.

And finally,

"July month, cause for celebration. 18th extremely significant."

This was the exact date Kelly's rather unexpected baby was due.

Reading the notes to this incredible message prompted Kelly to pick up the phone in a flurry of emotion and inform me about her special "spirit-predicted" baby.

Kelly scheduled a second reading with me when she was about eleven weeks pregnant. It's not my usual protocol to see someone so soon after a reading, but Kelly's circumstances were unusual enough that I made an exception. I was just as intrigued as she was to see if any more information would come through from the spirit world.

The reading began and once more, I became aware of the spirit of her late grandfather, Bob.

During the reading, the spirit world conveyed messages to Kelly about her developing baby. They reassured her that she was not going through all this change alone. They were close by, watching over her and accompanying her to all of her medical appointments.

Kelly's relationship with the father was brief, and he made it clear he didn't want to be involved with the baby. Knowing that her relatives where accompanying her to appointments gave great comfort to Kelly.

Just then, Kelly's loved ones in spirit rushed forward and told me that they would all be with her at exactly three o'clock that very afternoon.

"Have you got a medical appointment at three o'clock today?" I asked.

"Yes, I have a baby scan this afternoon at three!"

Her loved ones in spirit assured Kelly that the absence of the father would have no impact on her future or that of her baby.

Before the end of the reading I was shown a baby scan, it was blue.

"I'm being told that you're having a baby boy, and that he'll be named after someone in the spirit world."

Kelly mentioned that even though she could only ever imagine having a girl, the one boy's name that she'd ever considered was Bobby, after her grandad Bob.

There were many more details that came through from the spirit world that morning, but most remain personal to Kelly.

It would be nine more weeks before the sex of Kelly's baby would finally be confirmed. As predicted, a little boy grew, developing perfectly in preparation for his arrival into this world.

Over a year later, I met up with Kelly and was at last introduced to baby Bobby. It was amazing to meet him, knowing that his birth had been preordained by Sprit. To look into his baby blue eyes, and say, "We knew all about your arrival before you were even conceived, we even knew your name," was quite an experience.

Spirit not only predicted Kelly's baby, but they also gave the exact name of the father before he and Kelly had met, the exact sex of the baby, down to his due date and name.

When information like this is given by Spirit, you have to ask how they know what lies ahead with such precision.

This experience certainly opens up many questions about this world and the next.

If Spirit can give information about the future that is this precise, could it mean the future has already been set?

Could it be possible that we are all just following a spiritual script that has already been written?

If so, what does this mean for free will if our decisions and choices have already been made?

This one experience raises some profound questions about the future and personal responsibility, which I will leave for now and perhaps include in a later book.

CHAPTER 17

Hell, Suicide, & Evil Spirits

Hell is a place many people fear is their eternal destination if they do not follow a certain religion or live their life according to a set of Bronze Age rules.

Many religious people believe that if you do not follow their particular religious teachings and moral code, then something extremely unpleasant will happen to you when you die.

You'll go to Hell.

Various religious texts describe Hell as a place of eternal suffering, weeping, and torment, with fire and burning sulphur, where the smoke of anguish will rise forever.

Who wouldn't be afraid of going to a place like this?

The fear of such a terrifying afterlife has kept many people from leaving these old myths and superstitions in the past where they belong.

This type of suffering portrays a physical view of what is waiting for those who don't behave in this world when they die.

However, the essential point to understand is that the spirit world is *non-physical.*

When we die, we leave the physical body behind, where it is buried or cremated. We no longer need our bodies for the next part of our journey, which is a spiritual one. It is impossible to endure any kind of physical suffering without the body. Therefore, no suffering of this kind can take place in the afterlife.

But, what if Hell is a place made purely of emotional suffering?

Emotional suffering is something I have come across an awful lot in **this** world, not the next.

Spirit people repeatedly give accounts of reunions with their loved ones on the other side, and describe the peace and love that surrounds them. I have never connected with a spirit person who speaks of any kind of emotional punishment taking place in the spirit world.

But what about religion in the spirit world?

With so many different religions on offer and almost all of them claiming to be the one true one, which of them is really practiced in the afterlife?

They can't all be right, surely?

I have delivered thousands of messages from spirit people who were particularly religious while here in the physical world.

Never once has a spirit person come through and tried to impose their religion on either myself or the sitter.

In fact, they appear to have left religion behind.

In the spirit world, there is no religion.

I've also never had the experience of a spirit person coming through and saying, "Hello Love, it's Mum. Sorry your dad can't be here, he went to Hell because he didn't believe."

Never has that happened.

In Spirit, there is no religion.

And more importantly, there is no Hell, either. That's right,

Hell does not exist!

What about Suicides?

Most people have a connection to either family or friends who have experienced the tragedy of suicide. The everlasting grief for those people isn't helped by the widely held belief that suicide is morally wrong, a belief that stems from religious teachings.

However, the idea or belief that those who have taken their own lives are somehow punished for it in the afterlife is almost universal and not merely a belief of the religious.

This is evident from the countless questions I receive on the subject:

- "Is it true that suicides aren't allowed to be with their families on the other side?"
- "Are those who take their own life held back in the spirit world and unable to progress?
- "Are they trapped in limbo or purgatory in the after-life?" (This is the question I am most frequently asked).

Perhaps it will comfort you to know the answer to all of the above questions is, "No!"

Those who pass by suicide are with loved ones in spirit, they seem content and secure. They are certainly not trapped in limbo or purgatory.

Do those who pass by suicide ever regret their decision? Sometimes they do. Once in spirit, they have the opportunity to reflect on their life and the decisions they have made, just as we can while we are here. I did have one experience where a young woman, who had just taken her own life, immediately regretted her decision because she hadn't intended on actually killing herself. Her attempt to scare her friends in a desperate cry for help resulted in her immediate transition to the afterlife. "I didn't mean it," she kept saying to me.

I've had many connections with those who have taken their own lives, and they advise in the strongest possible language that those in this world should never follow in their footsteps.

Why?

Because there is a reason for every life.

One Sunday afternoon, I had been asked at very short notice if I could step in to take the service at a Spiritualist church. The medium who had been booked to do the service was running late, and would never make it on time.

As I stood on the platform and delivered spirit messages to the congregation, I felt particularly drawn to one woman sitting near the front. She had a strong spirit presence around her. Every time I glanced at her during the service, I could feel strong emotions surrounding her. This poor woman sat alone with a look of total emptiness in her eyes.

I could feel her need to connect with someone, and each time a spirit came forward to communicate, I hoped they would be for her. But, no message came.

When the service was over, I stepped off the platform intent on leaving right away. But as I passed the woman, the spirit presence around her grew stronger. It was the presence of a young woman who had taken her own life, a presence so strong I couldn't ignore it, nor could I leave the room without speaking to her. I approached the woman. She sat staring at the empty platform with a look of despondency on her face.

"Are you okay?" I asked.

She looked at me with great weariness and said, "When you were on the platform, I had the feeling there was something special about you. I really thought my daughter might come through, but . . ." Tears rolled down her face and her emotions prevented her from saying any more.

Instantly I knew her daughter in spirit had drawn me to her. Impulsively I said, "I'm going to come to your home as soon as possible and conduct a reading for you. What your daughter needs to say has to be given privately."

We exchanged details and after arranging the appointment, I soon visited the woman at her home. As I walked down the garden path toward the door, I felt a sensation from the spirit world that I hadn't felt before, a real feeling of urgency.

Once inside, we sat at the dining room table and the reading started immediately. My connection with the spirit world was loud and clear.

"I have your daughter here and the message she has for you is very important. She's telling you NOT to take your own life. Stop saying you're going to join her."

"Oh my God, that's true. She knows." The woman wept heavily into her handkerchief.

I continued, "She saw you sitting on the bed this morning holding a lock of her hair. She knows you are struggling with the grief of losing her to suicide, but you mustn't take your own life. She loves you and it's not your fault."

The woman nodded in agreement as she wiped tears from her eyes and blew her nose.

"She tells me she has a brother who she watches over."

"Yes, Matthew, my son. He's very close to her as well."

"Your son loves you and needs you. He's at a very critical point in his life right now. He already lost his sister, losing his mum at this stage could destroy him."

The young woman in spirit explained how she had gone through such a distressing and turbulent divorce that she had become consumed with depression. And it was this depression that led to her suicide.

"Mum, I'm okay. I'm with Grandad and Grandma. I can see so clearly from here. I realize now that I didn't have to take my life. It wasn't necessary."

After receiving evidence of her daughter's survival in the afterlife, this heartbroken mother now has a glimmer of hope. Her focus shifted from wanting to end her life to wanting to help her son. Relieved that her daughter was safe and well with her grandparents in spirit, this woman could now begin a new chapter in her life. What an important message from the afterlife.

I couldn't help but wonder, if the other medium hadn't cancelled, would this message still have been delivered? Or was it a lifesaving synchronicity from the spirit world?

At the time, the young woman had no idea just how much of an impact her passing would have on the people she loved in this world. Her depression blinkered her from seeing that. Breaking the hearts of her loved ones was the last thing she ever wanted to do.

For most of us, it is very difficult to imagine the depth of someone's emotional suffering to the point where they can see no way forward other than ending their life. I can only imagine how much a person must be suffering in order to do that.

However, I can say with confidence that those who choose to end their life in this world are not punished for it in the next. They are not held back, kept from their loved ones, or prevented from progressing spiritually. All are welcomed with love into the afterlife. That being said, those in the spirit world who have passed by suicide continue to express the importance of the life we have in this world. Every life is precious to someone, and everyone is precious to Spirit.

Evil Spirits

Connecting with the spirit world is an everyday experience for me. It is something I have done since childhood. However, every so often I will come across someone who has no experience with Spirit at all, but that doesn't seem to stop them from giving me their "advice" or their opinions on it.

I've lost count of the number of times I have been warned that I'm dabbling with the unknown, or that I'm opening the door to evil spirits that can never be closed. Some views are even more extreme than that, going so far as to say that I'm actually in contact with demons or evil spirits who are just pretending to be our loved ones on the other side.

For thousands of years, evil has been defined by religion and the religious as pure wickedness, something that thrives off fear and wants to control, dominate, and rule by any means it can.

A constant battle between good and evil taking place in the spirit realm is an old-fashioned idea that can be found in many ancient myths. But, not only is this not true, it is actually impossible.

Spirit is unconditional love.

Unconditional love has to love everything without exception, otherwise it wouldn't be unconditional. This means it cannot oppose anything or anyone. It would be impossible for unconditional love to engage in an act of violence or vengeance, for a battle in any given form would mean favouring one side over another, which it cannot do.

If evil did exist in the spirit realm, it would be the only thing that existed because unconditional love doesn't fight. Good would be overthrown immediately without a battle.

This means that not only do evil spirits not exist, they can't exist.

CHAPTER 18

The Afterlife

Mediumship provides us with evidence of an afterlife. When our loved ones come through to pass
on their messages, it is evident from the things
they say just how pleasant life is on the other side.

Once we are assured as to their wellbeing and happiness, our
attention naturally turns from *how* they are to *where* they are.

Where do we go when we die?

What is the afterlife like?

And who will be there?

When spirit people come through from the other side, whether
in a private one-to-one reading or a public demonstration, they
frequently pass on information about their life on the other side.

They share amazing details about people they have met, things they have seen, ailments that have disappeared, and sometimes descriptions of where they are in the spirit world.

Some spirit people talk about having a bungalow, or a house by the sea, others talk about tending their gardens and even growing vegetables in a greenhouse. Each unique individual who comes through from the other side gives an equally unique description of what life is like for them in the spirit world. It would seem that the place each person goes to is exactly what they hoped or imagined it would be.

Could it be that each person gets their own individual version of the afterlife?

In this book, I share a story about a woman who told her mum that if there were such a thing as heaven she would be there, drinking red wine and eating a pizza. When she came through in the reading, that's exactly what she was doing.

Was this really a vision of the afterlife, or was it her way of saying heaven is real?

During a family reading I gave in America, a young man came through who loved baseball. He told his loved ones that he was having a great time meeting all the baseball greats in the spirit world that he'd admired during his life time. He could not have asked for a better afterlife.

One spirit lady described walking through fields of beautiful flowers in spite of losing both of her legs in this world. Spirit people often describe being free from any illness, ailments or disabilities they had in this life. After all, these are conditions that come with having a physical body, and there is no physical body in Spirit. There is no illness in Spirit, nor is it possible to endure any kind of physical pain.

Despite the many different descriptions of the afterlife there is one account given by almost all spirit people that remains consistent, and that is of what happens at the point of death. Whether it's a long-term illness, suicide, or a sudden passing, the account they give remains the same.

At the point of death, they experience an overwhelming feeling of peace and love. It is more intense than anything they've ever experienced before. A beautiful warm feeling of relaxation washes over them. They see their loved ones, family members, and friends who have previously passed away gathered around them. Everybody is welcomed into the spirit world by somebody who is special to them. Nobody goes alone.

All worry ceases.

All stress melts away.

The next journey of life begins.

Leaving the physical body behind brings up a number of interesting questions about the afterlife.

If we no longer have a body, what will we look like?

And how do spirit people see without eyes?

Hear without ears?

Or touch without hands?

These are questions that have been put to me over the years by many different people, and as always, I put them to Spirit for the answers. So how will we continue to experience life without the body?

Well, you actually experience this every night when you sleep. Think about it.

Every night when you sleep, you dream.

In your dreams you can see people in the greatest of detail, but you don't use your eyes, they are shut. You can also have full conversations with people in your dreams. You hear every word they say, but you don't use your ears. In your dreams, you can run and jump, touch and hug, eat and drink, but you don't use your body, it's asleep in your bed.

When you enter the dream world, you see without your eyes, hear without your ears, and touch without your hands. You are experiencing a different kind of reality whilst in a different state of consciousness. Similarly, when we pass over to Spirit it will be a shift from one conscious state to another. You will experience a very different kind of reality, just as you do in the dream world.

There is another aspect to dreams that I find truly amazing. Once you grasp this, you'll never look at your dreams in the same way again.

Each night as you drift off to sleep you experience the dream world. As you wander through your dream, your mind creates new and powerful experiences. The incredible thing about dream phenomena is that you create the dream, and you experience it at the same time. You are experiencing your own creation and your consciousness does this so perfectly you don't even realize you are doing it.

Just think about the sheer volume of detail that your mind creates in your dreams; buildings, cars, people, animals, and vast landscapes. Not to mention all of the emotions that go along with the dream experience.

When our mind is in the dream state, we travel between two worlds.

During the writing of this book, I had one of the most incredible experiences whilst drifting between this world and the next.

I woke to find myself in the most beautiful landscape I had ever seen. I stood on top of rugged hills looking out at the ocean. This landscape looked similar to the Scottish highlands and had the beauty of Glen Nevis. In the ocean, beautiful jagged mountains where spiking up out of the water. I stood there in awe observing this incredible scene as snowflakes quietly fell on top of those mountains. It was so picturesque that I wished the snow would fall where I stood. The second that thought entered my mind, beautiful snowflakes began to fall gently all around me. It was cool but not cold, I held out my hands and watched the snowflakes landing on my fingertips.

I walked along the edge of the hilltop overlooking the ocean. I could feel the cool air in my lungs and hear the sound of the snow crunching beneath my feet. It was more vivid than anything I've ever experienced in the waking world. But, more powerful than the beauty of this place was the feeling inside me. Words cannot even begin to describe the depth of peace I felt, or the love that engulfed my entire being. No fear, no worry, just a feeling of pure harmony. This was a glimpse of what the afterlife will look like for me.

I wasn't dreaming about the spirit world, I was there.

When I woke from this experience, I was completely over-whelmed with emotion. I didn't want to come back. For days afterwards I could do nothing but dwell on this place. All I could think about was how to get back there. Life in this world felt so heavy after having this experience. Even though I am happy in my life, nothing compares to the feeling I had whilst I was there. I cannot wait for the day that I go back.

If our consciousness can create an entire world as we sleep, just think what it could do when it is free to explore the spirit realms. Countless worlds and experiences could be created as your consciousness expands and you become more spiritually evolved. This may be one reason we get so many different reports of what the afterlife is like.

If the dream world is different for everyone, then perhaps the spirit world is too, with each one of us creating our own personal versions of the afterlife, just as we do in our dreams.

There is a parallel that can be drawn with the dream world and the afterlife.

Nothing in the dream world is physical, but whilst we are there, it appears to be just as real as this one. Usually, it is only when we wake up that we realize we were dreaming. Everything you touched or held in the dream world has to remain there when you wake up, nothing physical can be brought back. While the dream itself may not be real, the experience of it undoubtedly is. And it is the experience of the dream that you bring back.

Nothing else.

Similarly, when you die, everything you have in this world will be left behind. Your house, car, life savings, everything. Nothing physical can be taken into the afterlife. The only thing you take with you from this world is the experience of it.

If the only thing we take with us is our experience of this life, then that can be the only reason we're here.

Experiencing life is the meaning of life.

CHAPTER 19

Do Flies Have an Afterlife?

I n September of 2014 I returned to a café in the small Lancashire town of Darwen, a quaint little town with a great deal
of history.

The previous day, I'd had a long but enjoyable time putting up
posters for my upcoming demonstration of mediumship at the
local theatre. I finally arrived at the last shop in town and boy
were my feet aching. I asked the manager if he wouldn't mind putting up a poster in the shop window and he kindly said yes.

As he placed the poster in the window, he asked when I would
be appearing at the theatre.

"I'll be here on the fifth of September." I said.

He glanced at the poster he'd just displayed.

"Are you sure? That's not what it says on the poster. It says the fifteenth on here."

As I gaped at the poster, he was right. It did say the fifteenth. After all that work, it wasn't until I'd reached the last shop in town before I discovered the mistake. I would have to come back the next day and replace every single poster.

But, everything happens for a reason.

Had it not been for that mistake I would not have had the following encounter:

I was just in the process of removing one of the misprinted posters from a café window when the woman behind the counter looked at me, and immediately her eyes lit up in recognition.

"Is that you on the poster?" she asked.

"Yes, that's me."

She asked a number of questions about mediumship, spirits, and life after death.

As I answered her questions, a young girl popped up from behind the counter and said, "Do flies have an afterlife?"

"Oh, trust you to ask something like that," the woman said.

"Well I'm only asking," replied the young girl.

As this girl was at work with Mum in the café serving food, I presumed the very moment a fly announced its presence in such an environment it would be swatted from this life and into the next. You can't have flies buzzing around a café.

For a few seconds I stood there and tried to give the young girl an answer but I couldn't.

I was stumped.

"Actually, I don't know if they do or not, but when I find out I'll let you know."

Ever since then, I've been determined to find an answer for that young lady.

At first, it may seem like a simple question to answer, and it would have been easy to say, "No, they don't." However, that wouldn't have answered the real question being asked here.

In her innocence, that young lady had opened up a deep and philosophical question.

In other words: Do life forms that are different from us also survive death?

Now that is a very profound question indeed.

We can't put life into different groups and say that this life survives death and this one doesn't. Nor can we say that one life is more important than another when it comes to the survival of the spirit. Something either has life or it doesn't, and flies most certainly do.

If human consciousness lives on after the death of the physical body, it is reasonable to presume that other life forms do as well. For years, I have delivered countless messages to people from the other side, and a great number of those messages involve animals in the spirit world.

From cats and dogs, to birds and reptiles, you name it. If they have been special to someone, they have managed to show up in a spirit message.

The first time I can recall an animal being involved in a reading was back in my office at Ye Old Wench and Trinkets.

My client took her seat and I explained how the reading would proceed. I closed my eyes and waited for the sensation of the spirit people to come. I didn't have to wait long, the moment I felt a spirit presence I opened my eyes, but what I saw wasn't what I expected.

Seated at the side of this woman was the biggest Rottweiler I'd ever seen!

Ghost whisperer yes, but dog whisperer I was not.

I blinked and the dog was gone.

"I've just seen a huge Rottweiler right by your side," I said.

To my surprise the woman's eyes filled up with tears, I handed her a tissue and continued.

"I can see the name Bethany, there's a strong connection with this name." It was a clairvoyant image I could see written up in front of my eyes.

"That's her name, my dog, Beth. We had to have her put to sleep a few months ago." The woman sniffed into her tissue. "Awe my baby girl, she's still with me."

It was clear to see just how important the connection with Beth was for this woman. At first, I hadn't realized that Bethany was actually the dog's name. And I must admit when she told me it seemed like an odd name for such a huge beast of a dog. But to this woman, Beth was her baby. It was wonderful to see the joy and relief in her eyes after being reunited with her much-loved companion.

This woman had got from the spirit world exactly what she was hoping for, a connection with her beloved Rottweiler. As a medium, it taught me never to underestimate the importance of a communication from the other side regardless of what form of life is coming through.

During another public demonstration of mediumship, a young girl from the spirit world came forward with a message for her mother who sat in the audience. The girl gave the most accurate of details in her message including the colour of her eyes, the illness she had passed with and even the exact size of the boots she wore. She mentioned how Mum still had those very same boots in the hallway at home.

As her mother acknowledged these details in her message, I was shown a vision of this young girl in the spirit world. She walked alongside a beautiful white horse, leading it by its reins and stroking its face. She wanted her mum to know that the horse was with her and that they were both together on the other side.

As her mother smiled and wiped tears of joy from her face, she informed me that her daughter had owned a white horse while she was still alive and well in this world. The boots I mentioned in the hallway were actually her riding boots, and the white horse I'd seen had only recently passed away.

Not only was this one of the most beautiful messages from a child to her mother, it was also amazing evidence that the spirits of our beloved animals reunite with us in the afterlife. The family had been so upset to say goodbye to the horse that their daughter had loved, ridden, and cared for in her short life. To have both of them come through in a message together was all the evidence the girl's parents needed that life, regardless of what form it takes, goes on.

Every message that comes through from the spirit world has meaning to the correct recipient of that communication. And the more messages I give, the more I notice just how important animals have become to people in this world.

I remember being contacted by a lady who was beside herself with grief over the loss of her beloved Charlie, a beautiful green budgerigar.

I had previously conducted a private reading at her home. While at her house, it became obvious how much she loved her little green bird. She would sit on the sofa watching TV with Charlie on a cushion by her side. When it was time for bed, Charlie slept on the pillow right beside her in the double bed.

I must say that the little fella was very well looked after, but due to his age, he looked a little moth-eaten. It was obvious that he had, perhaps for the benefit of this caring lady, stayed in this world a little longer than he should have. Most of his feathers were missing, Charlie was an old man and balding.

After the reading, the woman said it was nice to hear from her mother but didn't know what she would do when the day came to say goodbye to Charlie.

Well, a few weeks after that reading, the lady came home to find little Charlie had made his transition to the spirit world. Beside herself with grief and blaming herself for leaving him alone, she contacted me to see if I could give her some answers.

It didn't matter to this woman that Charlie was a bird. All she could see was a life, a special companion that meant the world to her.

The importance of a life cannot be determined by its size or status in this world. Charlie's life may have been tiny, but the impact of his departure from this world was enormous to the individual who loved him. The bond and the love that lady had for him was just as real and as powerful as the love we share for our own family and friends.

I know for sure that little Charlie will be around his caring owner for as long as he is needed.

We can learn a great deal from the bonds we share and the love we receive from our animal friends. They have a magical ability to enrich our lives on so many levels.

Through the numerous connections I have had with the spirit world, I can say with absolute conviction that our beloved pets also survive death. The spirit that dwells within all living creatures is eternal. And the bond we share with our beloved animals, just like our loved ones, can never be broken.

I find it quite outlandish that humans, being one of the most recent species to arrive on the planet after millions of years of evolving life forms before us, have managed to come to the conclusion that life is all about us. And if this life is all about us then the next life must be as well.

This is not the case.

Spirit dwells in all life, not just human life.

In my pursuit of answering that young girl's question, I wondered just how far down the chain of life you can go before a living creature no longer has a spirit.

I have come to the conclusion that if something has the ability to die then it is alive, and if it's alive, Spirit is involved in some way.

Where there is life there is Spirit and where there is Spirit there is life.

Do flies have an afterlife?

Yes.

But not as we know it.

CHAPTER 20

Give Me a Sign

Your loved ones in spirit are always around you. You only have to think about them and immediately they are with you. They are able to pick up on your thoughts and feelings from the spirit world.

You can talk to them whenever you need to.

No medium is required for this.

Speak to them in the same way you did when they were here physically. You don't need to use any special words or perform any kind of spiritual rituals.

Just speak to them normally.

You can do this out loud or just in your mind. Either way, they will hear you. You may not be able to hear them respond, but it is possible to become more aware of your loved ones in spirit by learning how to recognize and interpret the signs they give you. These signs can be subtle, but once you are aware of them, you'll start to notice them more and more.

That Funny Feeling

The presence of Spirit is usually accompanied by a very distinctive feeling in the solar plexus. You've probably already experienced this without realizing what it was.

It's like a feeling of anticipation, butterflies or a slight nervousness.

Quite often people will experience this sensation just moments before they receive a spirit message from a medium.

You are more likely to experience the spirit feeling when you are relaxed, or whilst carrying out an everyday, mundane task. The reason for this is that we are more receptive to the presence of Spirit when our mind isn't occupied by any particular line of thought, the daydream state as I call it.

If you've ever been ironing, washing up, or hoovering and suddenly had a rush of butterflies in your stomach for no apparent reason, it is likely to be the presence of a loved one letting you know they are near.

Dreams

Have you ever had the experience of someone who has passed away visiting you in a dream? Or heard someone call your name as you drift off to sleep?

Dreams play a big part in spirit communication. As we drift off to sleep our mind unwinds, relaxes, and opens up. When we enter the dream state, our consciousness drifts freely between the two worlds.

In a dream visitation, spirit people appear just as real and life-like as they did in this world. You can see them, hug them, and hold conversations with them at great length. This kind of visitation from a loved one can be one of the most wonderful and up-lifting experiences.

If you are yet to experience this, here is a simple method that I often advise people to try;

Each night before you fall asleep, send out thoughts to the loved one you'd like to connect with. Ask them to come and visit you in your dreams. Relax while you do this, then allow yourself to drift off to sleep and see what happens.

Try not to be too disappointed if you wake and find that you cannot recall having a visitation. Sometimes we remember our dreams and sometimes we don't. When you are ready for this experience, it will happen for you.

Apports

Have you ever gone to the place where you always leave your keys to discover they are missing? Then, after searching all over for them you return to that same place only to find them staring you right in the face?

You know full well they weren't there a moment ago.

This is known as an *apport.*

Traditionally, apports are physical objects that materialize during séances.

They range from small everyday objects such as coins, keys, and items of jewellery, to the outright peculiar. Musical instruments and even live animals have been known to appear!

However, apport phenomena is not restricted to the séance room. It can happen at any location and at any time. Thousands of people have experienced items mysteriously showing up in their homes without any explanation as to how they got there. Just how Spirit manage to accomplish this is unknown, but materializing apports is yet another way that spirit people indicate their presence.

Of all the reported apports that have appeared, feathers and coins seem to be among the most common. Anything from little white feathers, to colourful exotic quills have appeared seemingly from nowhere. Coins from all parts of the world, even old currencies from the past have materialized. Usually their country of origin, or the date that they were minted is of some significance to the recipient of this spirit gift.

The next time you have an item mysteriously vanish, or appear, it could well be that you have just experienced apport phenomena.

Photographs

Moving photographs have been reported for decades. To find that the photo of a loved one in spirit has moved from its original position, or even moved to a completely different place altogether, is more common than you might think. A photo is an item that has captured the image of your loved one and naturally draws your thoughts to that person. A spirit person moving a picture of themselves is a sure-fire way of getting your attention. The next time you find a photo strangely out of place, take a good look at who appears in that picture, they may be closer than you think.

Other Signs

There are all sorts of subtle little signs the spirit world give to indicate their presence. Not everything they do is as obvious as a discarnate voice or physical materialization.

There are many occasions when I have sensed a distinctive aftershave or perfume around me, which hasn't come from any known source. Typically, it is a scent that can be associated with a particular individual on the other side.

I've had the smell of lavender, pipe tobacco, cinnamon and sweet-smelling flowers to name just a few. One afternoon while having a coffee and a chat at a friend's house, the living room suddenly filled with a powerful smell of apples. It lasted for around five minutes. Then just as quickly as it arrived, it was gone.

A gentle touch on the face, tap on the shoulder or stroke of the hair is something else that I, along with many other people experience in the presence of Spirit. These signs are gentle and subtle, but they undoubtedly occur.

Most spirit-related phenomena are spontaneous and happen when we least expect it. However, it does tend to occur more frequently when we are going through a difficult or emotional time in our lives. Spirit people always come to comfort, uplift, and reassure us at the times we need them most.

To receive a sign from a loved one in spirit, all you have to do is ask. When they are ready, they will find a way to make you aware of their presence. Don't be disheartened if you do not receive an immediate response to your request. When the time is right, the signs will come.

I always advise those who are looking for a sign from the other side to be patient and level-headed about it.

It is important to be sensible about the phenomena and not put every little happening down to a spirit presence or a sign from the afterlife. There are natural occurrences such as creaking doors, banging pipes, and flickering lights that happen quite naturally without the interference of the spirit world. Be open-minded, but also be real about it.

The phenomena I have covered in this chapter may be new to you, but now that you are aware of the signs and what to look for, I'm pretty sure it won't be long before you experience them.

Our loved ones in spirit are always close by, and by the very act of thinking about them, they are near.

CHAPTER 21

No Regrets

O ver the last thirty years, Spirit have taken me on an incredible journey; from the brink of death and back again in 1983 to delivering messages from the spirit world to thousands of people.

Not only have I lost my fear of the unknown, but I have lost my fear of death completely. Although I may not be looking forward to the method of my transition, when my time comes to leave this world I know for certain what is waiting for me on the other side; a beautiful reunion with everyone I have ever loved and lost.

Those who have experienced a personal message from the spirt world frequently report just how much it has changed their understanding of life after death. I have the privilege of delivering spirit messages as part of my everyday life. When you spend as much time as I do communicating with those who are already on the other side, all doubt regarding the afterlife disappears.

My time with the spirit world has not only removed my fear of death, but it has also removed my fear of life. So many of us are afraid to do what makes us happy for fear of what others may think.

From the moment we arrive in this world, the clock is ticking. It really is only a matter of time before we make our transition back to Spirit. This could be a daunting thought, but if I can encourage you to do one thing at all, that is to live your life the way *you* want to, with no regrets.

Remember, experiencing life *is* the meaning of life.

Live. Learn. Experience.

Mediumship is a powerful force. It has the power to reconnect us with our loved ones, to offer hope, alleviate grief, and prove beyond belief that love never dies. With that kind of reassurance, I hope you can see that life can and should be lived without regret.

We see it too often, don't we? When we lose a loved one, that's when we pull out the family photos and relive the "good old days" by sharing our memories, and declaring how much they meant to us when they were here.

Why wait until our loved ones are gone?

Do it now.

Today.

On the journey that Spirit has taken me, I have had the price-less opportunity to meet thousands of people, both from this world and the next. I have learned from their mistakes and their regrets, applying those lessons to my own life, and encouraging others to do the same.

Don't wait until they're gone to show them just how much you care.

This appears to be one of the biggest regrets I come across when meeting people on my journey. Your loved ones in spirit are only a thought away, but your loved ones on earth are only a phone call away.

You and your loved ones will get far more joy from sharing a ten-pound pizza surrounded by love and laughter today, than a ten-thousand-pound funeral after they've passed.

So dig out those photos, share those stories, and enjoy every minute of your time together.

Don't leave it too late.

That extra shift at work can wait, the housework will still be there in the morning. Pick up the phone right now and tell them just how much you love them.

Our time in this world is short, but believe me, the love you build here lasts forever.

Are you ready to believe?

Best wishes,

David

Lightning Source UK Ltd.
Milton Keynes UK
UKHW02f2251180318
319622UK00007B/337/P